Wall, Cheryl, 1955–
Country comforts :
quilts for casual living
2010.
33305223733787
mh   10/17/11

D0720079

COUNTRY COMFORTS

QUILTS for CASUAL LIVING

WITHDRAWN

Cheryl Wall

Martingale®
& C O M P A N Y

Dedication

To my parents, whose lives of creativity and service continue to amaze and inspire me.

Acknowledgments

This book would not have been written without the support and assistance of the following people. My immense gratitude to:

Jeanne Preto, machine quilter extraordinaire—your expertise and suggestions for finishing my quilts were always right on the mark.

My Monday night quilting group, the Phat Quarters—you were with me when I took a deep breath and quit my day job to do this full time. Thanks for believing in me even when I didn't.

My dear, good friend Allyson—our long talks over tea helped to keep things in perspective when life got a little crazy.

The wonderful people at Martingale & Company—thank you for your support, advice, and for giving me the opportunity to cross one more item off my "bucket list"!

And finally, those of you who have bought my patterns and in so doing have encouraged me to continue doing what I do—it is because of you that I am able to follow my bliss.

Thank you.

Mission Statement

Dedicated to providing quality products and service to inspire creativity.

Country Comforts: Quilts for Casual Living
© 2010 by Cheryl Wall

That Patchwork Place® is an imprint of Martingale & Company®.

Martingale & Company
20205 144th Ave. NE
Woodinville, WA 98072-8478 USA
www.martingale-pub.com

No part of this product may be reproduced in any form, unless otherwise stated, in which case reproduction is limited to the use of the purchaser. The written instructions, photographs, designs, projects, and patterns are intended for the personal, noncommercial use of the retail purchaser and are under federal copyright laws; they are not to be reproduced by any electronic, mechanical, or other means, including informational storage or retrieval systems, for commercial use. Permission is granted to photocopy patterns for the personal use of the retail purchaser. Attention teachers: Martingale & Company encourages you to use this book for teaching, subject to the restrictions stated above.

The information in this book is presented in good faith, but no warranty is given nor results guaranteed. Since Martingale & Company has no control over choice of materials or procedures, the company assumes no responsibility for the use of this information.

Printed in China
15 14 13 12 11 10   8 7 6 5 4 3 2

Library of Congress Cataloging-in-Publication Data
Library of Congress Control Number: 2010003687

ISBN: 978-1-56477-996-0

Credits

President & CEO • Tom Wierzbicki
Editor in Chief • Mary V. Green
Managing Editor • Tina Cook
Developmental Editor • Karen Costello Soltys
Technical Editor • Nancy Mahoney
Copy Editor • Sheila Chapman Ryan
Design Director • Stan Green
Production Manager • Regina Girard
Illustrator • Laurel Strand
Cover & Text Designer • Regina Girard
Photographer • Brent Kane

CONTENTS

INTRODUCTION

When I made my first quilt over 25 years ago—a "Trip around the World" pattern designed to be completed in one weekend—I never suspected that first project would lead to a passion for quilting that would (almost) take over my life.

After that first project, I made a few quilts using templates, and when the rotary cutter and the speed of strip-piecing came along, that became my focus for awhile. My first quilts were copied *exactly* from patterns in books and magazines, trying to find the same fabrics, or at least the same colors, as in the photographs. As I grew more confident in my quiltmaking, I began choosing more of the fabrics I personally loved—rich, warm, dark colors and lots of contrast. Today, these are still the fabrics which first catch my eye.

I'm drawn to the primitive style of quilting and crafting because of the freedom it allows me to make projects that are less than perfect but still beautiful. I believe that the creative process should be fun and soul satisfying. Since I quilt for enjoyment and not for competition, I don't sweat the small stuff. If you look closely at my quilts, you'll likely find stars with rounded points and occasional seams that don't quite match. I think the little "mistakes" are what give quilts their charm and honesty. I want my creations to look unique and handmade, not mass produced. Although I continue to be awed by the painstaking attention to detail in

the prize-winning quilts I've seen at shows, and while I greatly admire the patience and precision required to produce these works of art, I know that's not my particular style. To strive for it would rob me of much of the joy I find in quilting. I believe we each need to discover the individual style that suits us best and celebrate it.

I hope this book reflects my relaxed, casual approach to quiltmaking. When I design a quilt, I don't cut all the pieces first and I don't necessarily use the quickest method to make the project. I like to choose colors and fabrics as I go along, which gives me the freedom to experiment and change direction. I love being surprised when the finished quilt turns out much differently than what I first intended. For this reason, I hope that these patterns will be a starting point for you and that you'll feel free to try your personal favorite colors and combinations when making them. I also feel that perhaps now more than ever, we need to bring joy into our lives and into the lives of those around us. I love designing patterns with that in mind.

This book is not intended to teach you how to make "perfect" quilts. But if you want to make quilts for the pure joy of creating, if you want to enjoy the journey not just the destination, and if this book gives you the freedom to make "mistakes" (and not feel obligated to automatically rip them out!), it will have served its purpose.

The Basics

In this section you'll find what you need to know to get started making quilts. If you're already familiar with the basics, use this section as a guide for any specific techniques used in the project you're making.

Supplies

When you're just starting to make quilts, choosing your supplies can seem overwhelming—there are so many choices out there! These are the tools I have in my sewing room. Use the list as a guide and add to it later, if you like.

- **Cutting mat.** Buy the largest mat you can afford! When using your rotary cutter, don't press down too hard on the mat and try to vary the lines you're cutting on; this will help keep the surface of the mat from getting too worn in one spot. Never roll your mat or leave it in direct sunlight.
- **Design wall.** A white flannel sheet tacked to a wall is fine. It really helps to choose fabrics if you can place the pieces you're considering next to each other, and then step back a few feet to see them from a distance.
- **Mechanical pencil.** A mechanical pencil with a .5 mm lead works great for making light marks on fabric.
- **Fine-tipped permanent marker.** Use this for signing your quilts.
- **Freezer paper.** Ordinary freezer paper, found at your supermarket, is ideal for making appliqué templates.
- **Iron and ironing board.** Choose an ironing-board cover that is flat, not puffy.
- **Masking tape.** Use wide tape for securing quilt backs to a floor or table when basting and narrow tape as a guide for hand quilting straight lines.
- **Needles.** Size 80/12 needles work well for machine piecing. For hand quilting, I prefer a #5 embroidery needle, which is a larger than a typical quilting needle, for ease of threading and because my stitches tend to be on the larger side.

- **Rotary cutter.** Use a rotary cutter with a sharp blade (45 mm or larger). When the blade gets dull, keep it to cut paper for other craft projects.
- **Rulers.** I like to use a 6½" square ruler for working with small pieces of fabric and a 12½" square ruler for cutting larger pieces. In addition, I use a 6" x 24" ruler for making long cuts for strips and borders. All of the rulers are clear acrylic with ⅛" increments and 45° lines marked on them.
- **Safety pins.** I use 2"-long pins for pin basting before quilting and smaller pins for pinning appliqué pieces to the background.
- **Scissors.** I keep one pair strictly for fabric use and another for cutting paper.
- **Seam ripper.** Yes, I do resort to using this occasionally!
- **Sewing machine.** If you can sew a straight stitch you can make my patterns!
- **Thread.** Buy good-quality thread—beige and black for patchwork will probably be enough for most projects. For appliqué, use thread that matches the appliqué pieces.
- **Washable marker.** Check the marker on a piece of scrap fabric first to make sure it will wash out properly. Don't iron any fabric that still has markings from a washable marker on it—doing so could leave a stain.

Fabric

In most cases, I don't specify fabric colors in the project instructions because I see these designs as a starting point in which you can experiment with your preferred palette. When purchasing fabrics, learn to trust yourself. Look around your house. What colors predominate in your decorating? I'm drawn to homespuns and rich colors, but you might prefer soft pastels or bright colors. If you love what you're working with, the process of creating is a lot more fun! Don't be afraid to try different combinations to make these designs your own. Use fabrics in your stash and let your quilts surprise you.

Fabric Selection and Preparation

I use 100%-cotton fabrics in my quilts, except for the projects where I also incorporate wool appliqué. Since I use a lot of scraps in my designs, and most of my quilts are for decorative use and probably won't need to be washed, I don't prewash my fabrics. If I'm concerned about color bleeding (usually with reds or older fabrics), I soak a corner of the piece in a cup of hot water for several minutes. If there's any color in the water after that time, I don't use that particular fabric in my quilt.

Instead of listing specific colors for some of the quilts in this book, I indicate light, medium, and dark fabrics, or light background fabrics. Light background fabrics can be muslin, light tan, beige, cream, or off-white. Dark fabrics are very dark blues, reds, greens, olives, browns, rusts, dark gold, and of course, black. Light colors refer to lighter shades of the same colors. Medium colors are those which don't absolutely fit into either the dark or light category.

Of course, color value varies depending on the colors and how they're combined in the fabric and also which fabric they will be placed next to in the quilt. When I'm not sure if there will be enough contrast between two adjacent fabrics, I "audition" the fabrics by placing them side by side on my design wall and stepping back a few feet for a better perspective. When I'm making flying-geese units, for example, I want to clearly see the shapes within the pieces. If the fabrics blend together too much, I don't use that particular fabric combination.

Don't be afraid to use the "wrong" side of the fabric in your blocks. I especially like to do this when using brushed cottons and I don't want the fuzzy side on top. As one shop owner told me, "You've paid for both sides—so use them however you want!"

Tea Dyeing Fabric

Several of these patterns use tea-dyed muslin, which I like because it gives the quilt an aged appearance. Since tea dyeing your muslin will cause it to shrink, dye it before cutting out the piece you need. You'll find it easiest to dye 10"-wide strips of muslin at a time. Here's my method for the blotchy tea-dyed look I like.

1 Put three or four tea bags in a large bowl; loosely scrunch the fabric and place it on top.

2 Pour hot water over the fabric until it's covered. After a few minutes, stir the fabric in the water and let the tea steep until the fabric's a bit darker than the color you want. (It will dry lighter.)

3 Rinse the fabric under cold running water, wring out the excess, and dry in the dryer or in the sun. Iron out most of the wrinkles.

Wool

I love the look of hand-dyed wool for its variation in color, which can add so much interest to a quilt. And wool is so much fun to work with! If your local quilt shop doesn't carry wool, check out the clothing section of your nearest thrift store. You can usually find women's skirts or coats or blankets that are still usable (be sure to check the label to make sure the item is 100% wool, or very close to it). Choose items that are not too heavy or too light. Cut them apart at the seams, remove any lining, and wash on a gentle cycle in your machine, using warm water and a bit of detergent. Dry the wool in your dryer and use it as instructed in the pattern.

Patchwork

I recommend reading all of the instructions before beginning each project to help you understand the various steps involved. And, unless otherwise stated, all seam allowances are ¼" wide and the fabrics are sewn right sides together.

Rotary Cutting

1 Before cutting, press your fabric to remove all creases and wrinkles. Fold the fabric in half lengthwise with the selvages aligned, hold the piece out in front of you, and make sure the fold is hanging straight. If there's any wrinkling or twisting along the fold, adjust the selvage edges by shifting them to the left or right. Lay the fabric on the cutting mat with the folded edge closest to you. Place a square ruler along the

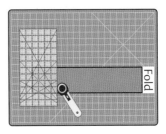

folded edge of the fabric. Line up a long ruler on the left-hand side of the fabric, covering just the uneven raw edges of the fabric. If you're left-handed, reverse this procedure.

squares or rectangles until you have the number needed.

❷ Remove the square ruler and cut along the right edge of the long ruler, rolling the rotary cutter away from you. Throw away this scrap of fabric.

❸ To cut strips from the fabric, align the cut edge with the correct width on the ruler. Always cut away from you and always close the rotary-cutter blade whenever you lay the tool down.

❹ To cut squares or rectangles, cut strips in the width specified in the project. Trim the selvage ends of the strips and align the left edge of the strip with the correct line on the ruler. Cut

When cutting homespun, plaid, or striped fabrics, cut on the straight of grain—regardless of whether it matches the lines on the fabric! Sometimes the pattern on the fabric is slightly off grain, which means that when you cut a straight-of-grain strip, you may end up with a piece in which the lines are slightly slanted. To me, this only adds to the quilt's charm.

Sewing and Pressing

Since I like to audition fabrics as I'm making my quilt, I prefer to not cut out all of the pieces ahead of time. This gives me the freedom to change the look of the quilt as I go. However, once I've chosen the fabrics for a certain block, I often save time by chain piecing. When sewing the pieces in a row together, I pair up the pieces and sew the pairs together in a long strip without removing them from the machine.

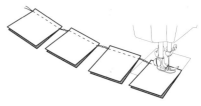

Then I cut the pieces apart, arrange them in rows again, and stitch the pairs together. This helps the quilt come together quickly without my having to commit to all the fabrics by cutting them first.

When pressing, don't press the seam allowances open—instead, press them to one side. As a general rule, press the seam allowances toward the darker piece. When matching the seam intersections, butt them together. Press the back of the pieces first to make sure the seams are smooth; then turn the pieces over and gently press the seams from the front. Lay the iron down gently on the piece and lift it up. Try not to stretch the fabric by "ironing" (wiggling the iron back and forth) or it might lose its shape.

When I sew a single piece of fabric to one that's pieced (such as a border to the quilt top), I keep the single fabric piece on the bottom next to the feed dogs. That way, as I'm sewing I can see the seams and seam intersections to make sure everything stays the way it's been pressed and doesn't get turned in the wrong direction.

Making Half-Square-Triangle Units

❶ Cut squares the size specified in the cutting list. Place two squares right sides together and sew diagonally from corner to corner. On squares that are 2½" or smaller, I usually estimate the stitching line. For larger squares, on the wrong side of the lighter square, use a pencil to lightly draw a line diagonally from one corner to the opposite corner, and then stitch on the drawn line.

❷ Trim away the excess fabric on one side, leaving a ¼" seam allowance as shown. Press the seam allowances toward the darker triangle.

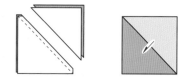

I rarely throw away any of my scraps. As I trim the excess fabric, I throw the bits into wire baskets I have close by, keeping similar colors together in each basket. These odds and ends come in handy when I'm making a scrap quilt that calls for a single piece of a certain color. I also use them for other craft projects, such as stuffing rag pillows or dolls.

Making Flying-Geese Units

❶ Cut squares and rectangles the sizes specified in the cutting list. With right sides together, place a square on one end of a rectangle. Sew diagonally from corner to corner across the square, as shown.

❷ Trim away the excess fabric, leaving a ¼" seam allowance. Press the resulting triangle open.

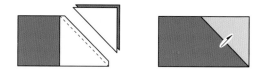

❸ Place a second square on the other end of the rectangle, right sides together. Sew diagonally across the square as shown. Trim the excess fabric, leaving a ¼" seam allowance, and press.

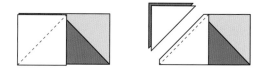

Appliqué

The first time I tried appliqué I swore I'd never do it again! I found it so frustrating to try to make the pieces look like the ones in the picture. It seemed like a crazy amount of work for something that didn't turn out right. But I did try it again and I'm so glad I did. Appliqué opens up so many possibilities for design and for adding your own personal touches to a quilt.

When you think about it, there are few (if any) identical shapes in nature—no two snowflakes are alike and I doubt that two roses, even if they are growing on the same bush, are exactly the same either. For this reason, my appliqué method allows for shapes to be a little different from each other, even when starting with the same template! Not worrying about having all the shapes identical gives my quilts the unfussy look I want. Here are my methods for appliquéing cotton and wool.

Cotton Appliqué

1. Trace each shape onto the dull paper side of freezer paper and cut out the shape on the marked line.

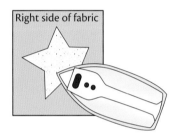

2. Press the freezer paper shiny side down onto the *right* side of the fabric.

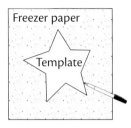

3. Cut out the appliqué shape, adding a ¼" seam allowance, and peel off the paper. Since you can reuse the freezer paper template several times, you don't have to cut a new template for each fabric piece.

4. For inside points and curves, you'll need to clip the seam allowance, but be careful to make the clip less than ¼".

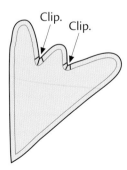

5. Referring to the quilt photo for placement, place the appliqué shapes on the background fabric or quilt top and pin them in place. Use a length of thread that matches the color of the appliqué piece; thread it through a needle and tie a knot in one end. The appliqué stitch is done right to left (or left to right if you're left-handed). Start on a straight edge of the appliqué piece and turn a section of the edge under ¼". Hold this edge with the thumb of your non-sewing hand as you bring the needle up through the fold, and then into the background fabric just in front of where the needle came out of the appliqué piece. Continue stitching around the appliqué piece, keeping the stitches small and close together.

6. To end your stitching, insert the needle under the appliqué piece and into the background fabric or quilt top to the wrong side. Make a couple of tiny stitches in the background, tie a knot, and clip the thread.

Wool Appliqué

1. Trace the appliqué shapes onto the dull paper side of freezer paper and roughly cut around the shape.

2. Iron the freezer paper shiny side down onto the wool. (Generally, washed wool won't have a right or wrong side, so choose the side you like to be the side that shows. Occasionally you'll find wool that does have two different sides, so it doubles your design options.)

3. Cut out each shape on the traced line (you don't need to turn the edges under) and peel off the paper. You can reuse the freezer paper templates several times.

4. Pin the wool shapes to the background and stitch in place using a blanket stitch or a whipstitch.

Embroidery Stitches

Embellishments can add a lot of interest to a quilt. Here are the embroidery stitches used for the projects in this book.

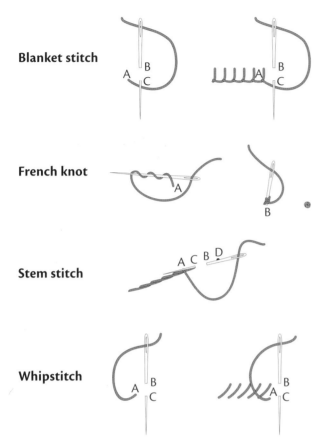

Blanket stitch

French knot

Stem stitch

Whipstitch

Borders

For the quilts in this book, most of the border strips are cut on the crosswise grain of the fabric, meaning that the border strips will have to be pieced together end to end to be long enough. The strips can be pieced with a straight seam or a diagonal seam to make the seam less noticeable. The measurements for the borders are *mathematically* correct if every block is cut and stitched perfectly. Since quilts, like life, don't always turn out perfect, here's how to measure the strips to make sure your quilt is square.

Fold the quilt top in half, aligning the top and bottom edges. In the center of the quilt top, measure from the fold to the raw edge. Multiply this measurement by two and cut two border strips to this length. Fold the strips in half and finger-press a crease to mark the center. Along the edge of the quilt top, mark the center with a pin. Match the

crease and the pin, and then pin the strip in place, matching the ends of the border strip and quilt. If necessary, stretch the edge of the quilt top a bit or ease in any excess to make it fit the length of the border. Sew the opposite border the same way. Then measure and sew the two remaining sides.

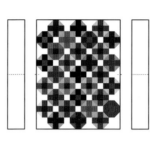
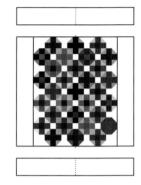

Finishing Your Quilt

Now that the quilt top is completed you're ready to move on to the final steps.

Quilt Backs

For the longest time, I would buy extra fabric for the back of the quilt, usually muslin or fabric that matched the quilt top. Then I realized that a quilt back is a great place to use fabrics I already have in my stash, or to include a block or two which was intended for the front but not used. Plus, piecing the back makes the quilt much more fun and interesting!

So, if I make a block or two for the quilt top but it doesn't work (maybe the color is wrong or I measured or cut it inaccurately), rather than throw it out, I try to use it on the back. First, I put these quirky blocks on my design wall, approximately where I want them on the quilt back and at least 6" from the outer edges, since these edges will eventually be trimmed away. Using a piece of fabric that coordinates at least a little bit with the quilt top and is a bit wider or longer than the block, I stitch the piece to one side of the block and trim away the excess to make both pieces the same width or length. I don't worry about measuring the pieces—I can always add or subtract more fabric later to get the finished dimensions I want. I just make sure the pieces are cut on the straight-of-grain to avoid stretching the fabric. Then, I sew another piece to the first piece, trim and so on, until the back of the quilt is finished. Press all of the seam allowances open and you're ready to layer your quilt.

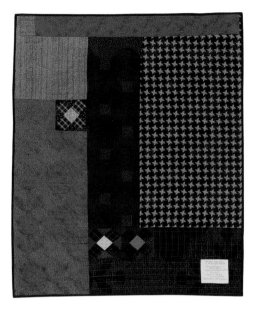

Back of "Autumn Equinox"—notice the blocks that didn't make it to the front! (See page 56 for the front of the quilt.)

Layering Your Quilt

I like to use thin 100%-cotton batting for my quilts, but you may prefer a cotton-and-polyester batting. Whatever you choose, follow the manufacturer's instructions to know how far apart to place your quilting stitches.

If your quilt is going to be finished on a long-arm quilting machine, ask the quilter how to prepare your quilt top, batting, and backing fabric. If you're going to hand quilt your project or machine quilt it on a regular sewing machine, you'll need to pin or thread baste everything first. I prefer pin basting because it takes less time than using thread and because I don't have to remove the basting thread when the quilt is finished.

1 Cut the backing fabric and the batting at least 4" larger on all sides than the quilt top. Lay the backing fabric wrong side up on the floor or a table. Use masking tape to anchor the edges. Center the batting over the backing, and then center the quilt top, right side up, over the batting. Starting in the center of the quilt top,

pin baste the layers together, working your way toward the outer edges. Place the pins about 6" apart, smoothing as you go.

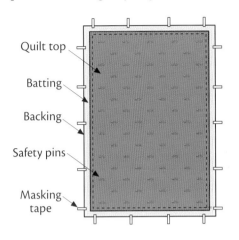

2 When you've finished pinning the layers together, remove the tape from the outer edge of the backing. Turn the quilt sandwich over and lay it out flat. Start in the center and smooth out any puckers, re-pinning the layers if necessary. Turn the sandwich over again to make sure the front is still pucker free. You might need to repeat this process several times before the quilt is completely smooth on both the front and back.

Quilting

When I have time to hand quilt, I use an 18"-diameter wooden hoop and stretch the center of my quilt inside it, removing any pins that are in the way. I prefer to use a #5 embroidery needle and take small stitches one at a time, straight up and down. Use whichever size needle and stitching method you prefer. I usually use quilting thread but occasionally, for a more primitive look, I use black pearl cotton, size 8, or two strands of embroidery floss.

When hand quilting straight lines, I use masking tape to mark where I want to quilt; however, if I'm following the seam lines in a pieced block, I usually eyeball it. For more elaborate quilting, I mark the design on the quilt top with a washable marker before layering. If I don't have time to hand quilt an entire top, I'll sometimes machine quilt along the seam lines to hold the layers together, and then add a bit of hand quilting in large spaces for interest.

Hanging Sleeve

Inserting a dowel into a hanging sleeve on the back of your quilt is a great way to hang your project on a wall. The quilt will hang straight and, because its weight is evenly distributed, the quilt is less likely to become stretched or misshapen over time. After the quilting is completed, I often have extra backing fabric that has been trimmed from one side that can be used to make a hanging sleeve. Or you can use a few different fabrics for the sleeve if you want!

1 Cut a strip that is about 4" longer than the quilt's width, piecing if needed, and about 8" to 10" wide. Fold the strip in half lengthwise, wrong sides together, aligning the raw edges.

2 On each end, fold the edges to the inside about 3" and press. Center the sleeve along the top edge of the back of your quilt with the raw edges aligned and pin in place. The top edge of the sleeve will be secured when you sew on the binding. Your quilt should measure about 1" wider than the sleeve on both ends.

3 After the binding has been attached, remove the pins from the sleeve. Keeping the sleeve flat against the back of the quilt; blindstitch the bottom of the sleeve to the backing fabric.

Binding Your Quilt

All of the binding for the quilts in this book were cut 2¼" wide across the width of fabric, and then pieced. If you prefer a wider binding, adjust the amount of fabric required accordingly.

1 Measure the perimeter of the quilt top and add 15" for seams and finishing corners. From the binding fabric, cut enough 2¼"-wide strips to total this measurement.

2 Sew the strips together at right angles, stitching diagonally across the corner to make one long strip. Trim the seam allowances to ¼" and press them open.

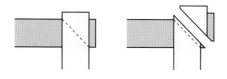

3 Cut one end at a 45° angle and press it under ¼". Fold the strip in half lengthwise, wrong sides together, and press.

4 Beginning with the angled end of the binding strip, align the raw edge of the strip with the raw edge of the quilt top. Starting near the middle on one side, and 1" from the strip's angled end, use a ¼"-wide seam allowance to stitch the binding to the quilt. Stop ¼" from the first corner and backstitch. Remove the quilt from the machine.

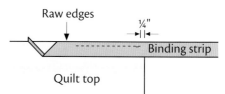

Raw edges
¼"
Binding strip
Quilt top

5 To turn the corner, bring the strip up, and then back down onto itself, aligning the raw edges on the second side. Begin with a backstitch at the fold of the binding and continue sewing down the second side. Stop ¼" from the next corner and backstitch. Continue around the quilt in this manner.

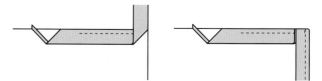

6 When you get close to the beginning of the binding, overlap the ends about 1" and cut off the excess fabric at an angle. Tuck the 1" inside the opening in the beginning binding strip. Continue stitching over the joined area, overlapping the beginning line of stitching.

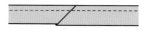

7 Trim the edges of the backing and batting even with the quilt top. Fold the binding over the raw edges and blindstitch in place so that the folded edge covers the row of machine stitching. At each corner, fold the binding to form a miter and stitch it in place.

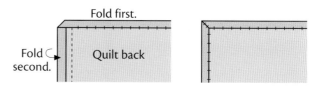

Fold first.

Fold second.

Quilt back

DAYS AND NIGHTS OF WINE AND ROSES

This quilt was inspired by the Okanagan Valley, an area in the interior of British Columbia, Canada, the province in which I live. It's known for its many vineyards, fruit orchards, and sandy lakeside beaches surrounded by hillsides baked gold by the hot summer sun. I tried to capture some of the Valley's richness in the colors of the fabrics and the appliqué designs I chose for this quilt.

Hints

This quilt is very scrappy, so I've designated fabric colors as black, dark, and light. But feel free to use a variety of fabrics to make up each of these categories. Use a variety of plaids, prints, and stripes, choosing them as you go, for a scrappy feel.

- For black fabrics, use a mix of your darkest blues, greens, and of course, black.
- For dark colors, use burgundies, greens, purples, and blues, a bit lighter than the blacks.
- For light colors, use cream, off-white, beige, pale gold, and other light background fabrics.

Materials

Yardage is based on 42"-wide fabric.

1⅜ yards *total* of assorted light fabrics for blocks

1¼ yards *total* of assorted dark fabrics for blocks and corner squares

⅞ yard *total* of assorted black fabrics for blocks and corner squares

⅞ yard of light fabric for outer border

½ yard of dark green fabric for vine, bud, and leaf appliqués

⅜ yard of dark burgundy fabric for heart, large flower, and bud appliqués

⅓ yard of black fabric for inner border

¼ yard *total* of assorted burgundy fabrics for small flower appliqués

¼ yard of gold fabric for star appliqués

¼ yard *total* of assorted purple fabrics for grape appliqués

⅝ yard of binding fabric

4 yards of backing fabric

67" x 67" piece of batting

Cutting

From the assorted light fabrics, cut a *total* of:
- 204 squares, 2½" x 2½"
- 116 rectangles, 1½" x 2½"

From the assorted dark fabrics, cut a *total* of:
- 136 squares, 2½" x 2½"
- 136 rectangles, 1½" x 2½"

From the assorted black fabrics, cut a *total* of:
- 252 rectangles, 1½" x 2½"

From the black inner-border fabric, cut:
- 5 strips, 1½" x 42"

From the light outer-border fabric, cut:
- 6 strips, 4½" x 42"

From the dark green fabric, cut:
- 1¼"-wide bias strips to total 210"

From the binding fabric, cut:
- 7 strips, 2¼" x 42"

Piecing the Blocks

This quilt is made using 11 different block variations, each consisting of squares and rectangles. The blocks are all essentially the same, but color placement makes each one a bit different, allowing you to assemble them in a Barn Raising setting. After sewing each seam, press the seam allowances in the direction indicated by the arrows.

Blocks 1 and 2

1. Pair four black rectangles with four dark rectangles and sew them together as shown to make four black/dark pieced squares. Pair three black rectangles with three light rectangles; sew them together to make three black/light pieced squares.

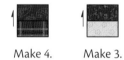

Make 4.   Make 3.

2. Lay out six dark squares, three light squares, and the pieced squares from step 1 in four rows as shown. Sew the squares together in rows, and then sew the rows together to complete the block. Make four of block 1 and four of block 2.

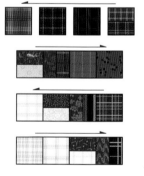

Block 1.
Make 4.

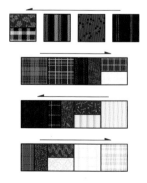

Block 2.
Make 4.

Blocks 3 and 4

1. Pair three black rectangles with three dark rectangles and sew them together lengthwise to make three black/dark pieced squares. Pair four black rectangles with four light rectangles; sew them together to make four black/light pieced squares.

2. Lay out three dark squares, six light squares, and the pieced squares from step 1 in four rows as shown. Sew the squares together in rows, and then sew the rows together to complete the block. Make two of block 3 and two of block 4.

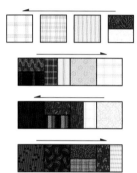
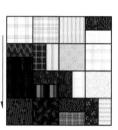

Block 3.
Make 2.

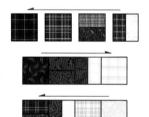

Block 4.
Make 2.

Pieced and appliquéd by Cheryl Wall. Machine quilted by Jeanne Preto.

Finished quilt: 58½" x 58½"

Finished block: 8" x 8"

Blocks 5 and 6

1 Pair three black rectangles with three dark rectangles and sew them together lengthwise to make three black/dark pieced squares. Pair five black rectangles with five light rectangles; sew them together to make five black/light pieced squares.

2 Lay out three dark squares, five light squares, and the pieced squares from step 1 in four rows as shown. Sew the squares together in rows, and then sew the rows together to complete the block. Make two of block 5 and two of block 6.

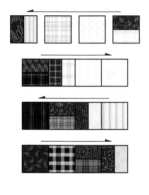

Block 5.
Make 2.

Block 6.
Make 2.

Blocks 7 and 8

1 Pair five black rectangles with five dark rectangles and sew them together lengthwise to make five black/dark pieced squares. Pair three black rectangles with three light rectangles; sew them together to make three black/light pieced squares.

2 Lay out five dark squares, three light squares, and the pieced squares from step 1 in four rows as shown. Sew the squares together in rows, and then sew the rows together to complete the block. Make four of block 7 and four of block 8.

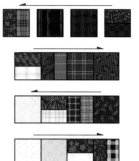

Block 7.
Make 4.

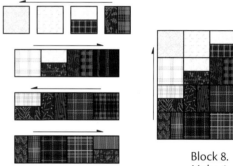

Block 8.
Make 4.

Blocks 9 and 10

1 Pair three black rectangles with three dark rectangles and sew them together lengthwise to make three black/dark pieced squares. Pair four black rectangles with four light rectangles; sew them together to make four black/light pieced squares.

2 Lay out three dark squares, six light squares, and the pieced squares from step 1 in four rows as shown. Sew the squares together in rows, and then sew the rows together to complete the block. Make four of block 9 and four of block 10.

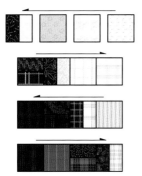

Block 9.
Make 4.

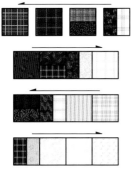

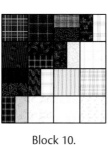

Block 10.
Make 4.

Block 11

Lay out 16 light squares in four rows as shown. Sew the squares together in rows, and then sew the rows together to complete the block. Make four of block 11.

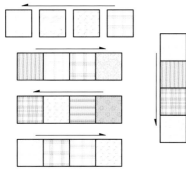

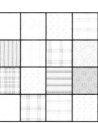

Block 11.
Make 4.

Assembling the Quilt Top

1 Lay out the blocks in six rows of six blocks each as shown. Sew the blocks together in rows. Press the seam allowances in opposite directions from one row to the next.

2 Sew the rows together and press the seam allowances in one direction.

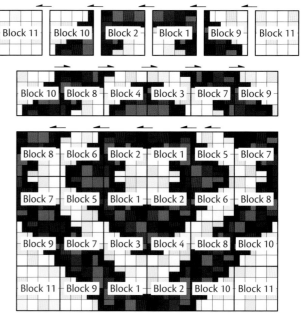

Quilt layout

Inner Border

1 Sew the 1½"-wide black strips together end to end. From the strip, cut two 48½"-long strips and two 50½"-long strips.

2 Sew the 48½"-long strips to the top and bottom of the quilt top. Then sew the 50½"-long strips to the sides of the quilt top. Press the seam allowances toward the just-added border.

Corner Blocks

1 Pair four black rectangles with four dark rectangles and sew them together lengthwise to make four black/dark pieced squares.

2 Lay out the pieced squares in two rows as shown. Sew the squares together in rows, and

then sew the rows together to complete the block. Make four corner blocks.

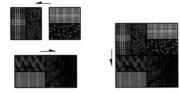

Make 4.

Outer Border

1 Sew the 4½"-wide light strips together end to end. From the strip, cut four 50½"-long strips. Sew a strip to the top and bottom of the quilt top. Press the seam allowances toward the border.

2 Sew corner blocks to both ends of the two remaining strips. Sew these strips to the

sides of the quilt top, matching the seam intersections. Press the seam allowances toward the border.

Appliqué

For detailed instructions, refer to "Cotton Appliqué" on page 9.

1 Using the dark burgundy, assorted burgundy, gold, dark green, and assorted purple fabrics and the patterns below and on page 20, cut out the appliqué shapes. Make the quantity indicated on the pattern for each shape.

Patterns do not include seam allowances. Add ¼" seam allowance for needle-turn appliqué.

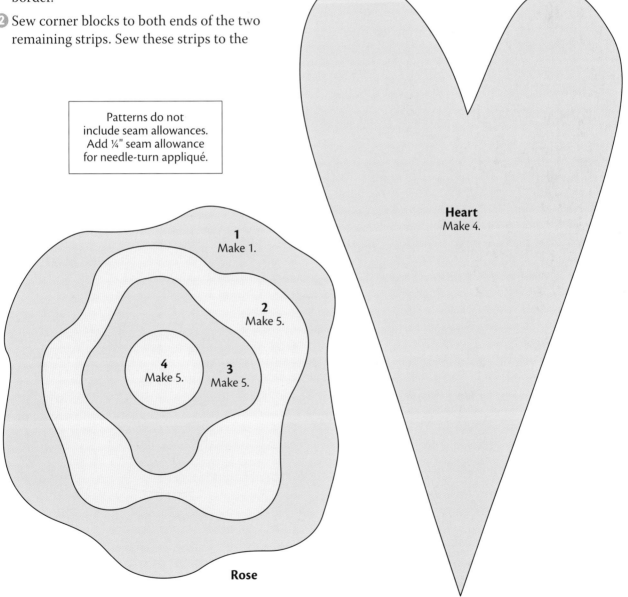

1 Make 1.
2 Make 5.
4 Make 5.
3 Make 5.
Rose

Heart Make 4.

2 For the vine, sew the dark green bias strips together end to end to make a long strip. Fold the strip in half lengthwise, wrong sides together, and sew a scant ¼" from the raw edges. Press the seam allowances to the back of the vine. Cut one strip about 130" long for the middle vine, four strips about 13" long for the corner vines, and two strips about 10" long for the center vine.

3 Using the photo on page 14 as a placement guide, pin the vines to the quilt top, trimming as necessary, and appliqué in place. Pin the remaining shapes to the quilt top so that they cover the short ends of the vine and appliqué in place.

Finishing

For detailed instructions on finishing your quilt, refer to "Finishing Your Quilt" on page 10. Using the 2¼"-wide binding strips, make and attach binding.

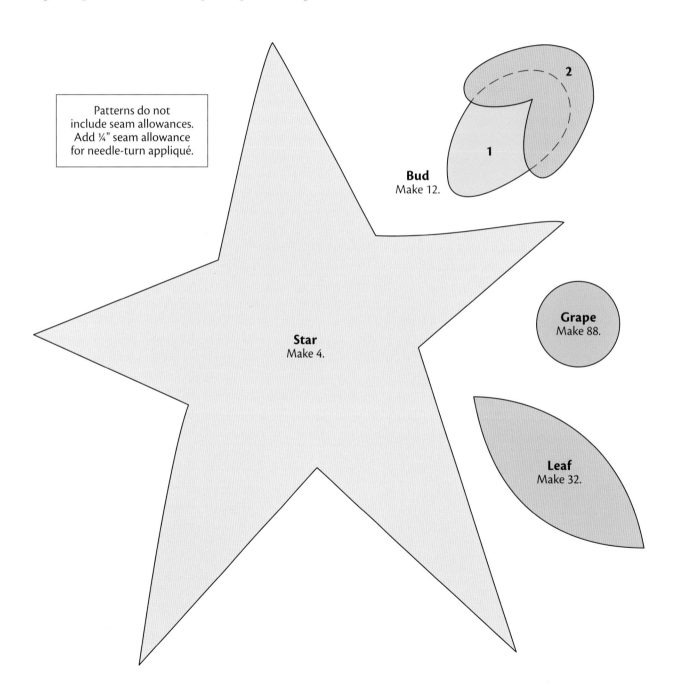

Patterns do not include seam allowances. Add ¼" seam allowance for needle-turn appliqué.

Bud
Make 12.

Star
Make 4.

Grape
Make 88.

Leaf
Make 32.

MOUNTAINS AND MEADOWS

This quilt was inspired by the Delectable Mountains block. The tea-stained muslin squares and large appliqué pieces give this quilt an aged and unfussy appearance, which I love. Appliqué pieces that aren't identical create a country charm and make the quilt fun to put together. It's also a great project for using fat quarters.

Hints

- If you want to tea dye the muslin like I did, do so before cutting the pieces. For detailed instructions, refer to "Tea Dyeing Fabric" on page 6.
- This quilt has lots of triangles with bias edges. Be careful not to stretch them when stitching or pressing.
- To add a little seasoning, include two or three red fabrics when choosing your assorted dark fabrics.

Materials

Yardage is based on 42"-wide fabric.

3 yards of muslin or other light background fabric for setting squares and border

2¼ yards *total* of assorted dark fabrics for blocks and flower appliqués

1⅛ yards *total* of assorted light or medium fabrics for blocks and flower-center appliqués

⅔ yard of dark green fabric for stem, vine, and leaf appliqués

⅜ yard of dark gold fabric for star appliqués

⅓ yard of dark red fabric for center circle and heart appliqués

⅝ yard of binding fabric

4½ yards of backing fabric

76" x 76" piece of batting

Tea (optional, for dyeing muslin)

Cutting

From the assorted light or medium fabrics, cut a *total* of:

- 12 squares, 4⅞" x 4⅞"; cut in half diagonally to yield 24 triangles
- 24 squares, 2⅞" x 2⅞"; cut in half diagonally to yield 48 triangles
- 96 squares, 2½" x 2½"

From the assorted dark fabrics, cut a *total* of:

- 12 squares, 8⅞" x 8⅞"; cut in half diagonally to yield 24 triangles
- 48 squares, 2⅞" x 2⅞"; cut in half diagonally to yield 96 triangles
- 120 squares, 2½" x 2½"

From the muslin or other light background fabric, cut:

- 36 squares, 8½" x 8½"
- 24 squares, 4½" x 4½"
- 48 squares, 2½" x 2½"

From the *straight grain* of the dark green fabric, cut:

- 2 strips, 1" x 13"
- 4 strips, 1" x 10½"

From the *bias grain* of the dark green fabric, cut:

- 4 strips, 1" x 19"
- 16 strips, 1" x 16"

From the binding fabric, cut:

- 8 strips, 2¼" x 42"

Piecing the Blocks

Directions are for making one block. Repeat to make a total of 24 blocks. After sewing each seam, press the seam allowances in the direction indicated by the arrows.

1. Refer to "Making Half-Square-Triangle Units" on page 8. Pair four 2½" light/medium squares with four 2½" dark squares; sew the pairs together to make four half-square-triangle units.

2. Sew two half-square-triangle units and a 2⅞" light/medium triangle together to make a strip as shown, keeping the top edge even. (The triangle point will jut out a bit at the bottom.

3. Sew a 2½" dark square, two half-square-triangle units, and a 2⅞" light triangle together to make a strip as shown, keeping the bottom edge even.

4. Sew the strip from step 2 to the short side of a 4⅞" light/medium triangle as shown. Then sew the strip from step 3 to the unit.

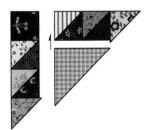 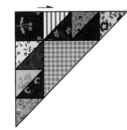

5. Sew the pieced triangle unit and an 8⅞" dark triangle together as shown to complete the block. Make a total of 24 blocks.

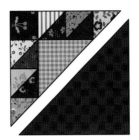

Make 24.

Piecing the Border Units

Directions are for making one border unit. Repeat to make a total of 24 units. After sewing each seam, press the seam allowances in the direction indicated by the arrows.

1. Sew two 2⅞" dark triangles and one 2½" muslin square together as shown. Make two of these units.

2. Sew the units from step 1 to adjacent sides of a 4½" muslin square as shown to complete the unit. Make a total of 24 border units.

 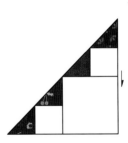

Make 24.

Designed, pieced, and appliquéd by Cheryl Wall. Machine quilted by Jeanne Preto.
Finished quilt: 68" x 68"
Finished block: 8" x 8"

Assembling the Quilt Top

1. Lay out the blocks, 8½" muslin squares, and the border units as shown. Sew the pieces together in diagonal rows. Press the seam allowances in opposite directions from one row to the next. Keeping the outer edges even, sew the rows together and press the seam allowances in one direction.

Quilt layout

2. Finish by machine basting around the quilt top a little less than ¼" from the outer edge to stabilize the seams, being careful not to stretch the pieces as you sew.

Appliqué

For detailed instructions, refer to "Cotton Appliqué" on page 9.

1. Using the dark, medium or light, dark green, dark gold, and dark red fabrics and the patterns on pages 26–28, cut out the appliqué shapes. Make the quantity indicated on the pattern for each shape.

2. To make the straight flower stems for the center of the quilt, along one long edge of a 1" x 13" green strip press about ¼" to the wrong side. Press the remaining long edge in the same way so that the raw edges just barely overlap. Prepare the remaining green straight-grain strips in the same manner. Referring to the photo on page 24 for placement guidance, pin the straight stems, leaves, center circle, stars, flowers, flower centers, and hearts in place on the setting squares, tucking the ends of the stems under the other shapes. Appliqué in place.

3. For the curved vine in the border, prepare the green bias strips as you did the straight stems. Using a washable marker and the vine placement guides on page 29, trace lines along each side and in each corner on the muslin border, again referring to the photo as needed. Pin the vines in place so that the inside edge of the vine follows the curve of the traced line. The ends of the vines will be covered by flowers. In the corners, slightly overlap the vines and turn under the raw end on the top vine. Appliqué in place.

4. Pin and appliqué the remaining flowers, flower centers, and stars to the muslin border.

Finishing

For detailed instructions on finishing your quilt, refer to "Finishing Your Quilt" on page 10. Using the 2¼"-wide binding strips, make and attach binding.

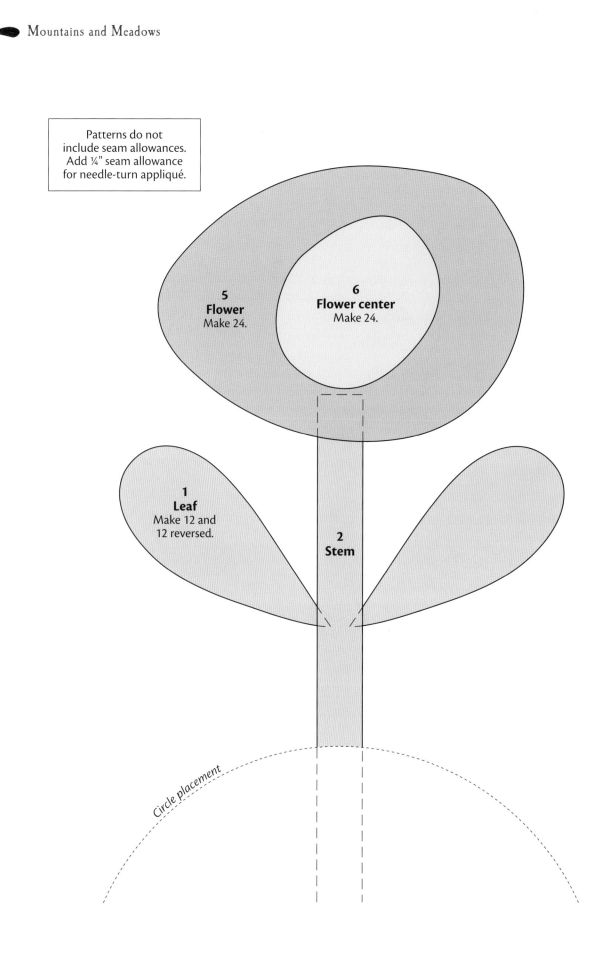

Patterns do not include seam allowances. Add ¼" seam allowance for needle-turn appliqué.

5
Flower
Make 24.

6
Flower center
Make 24.

1
Leaf
Make 12 and
12 reversed.

2
Stem

Circle placement

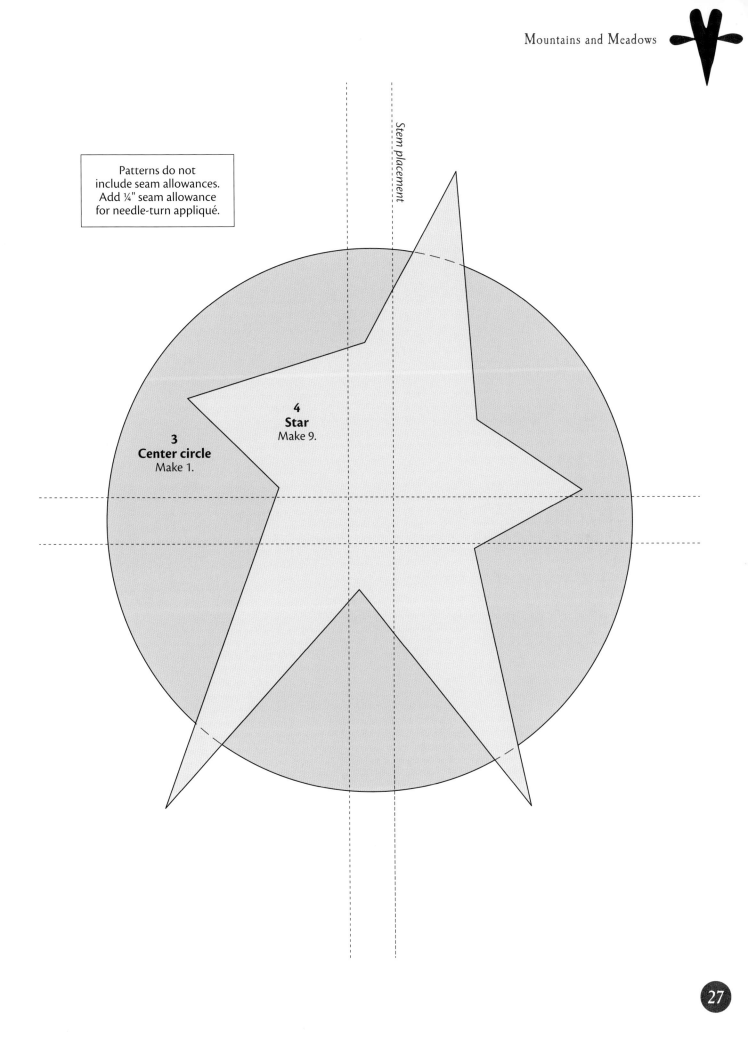

Stem placement

Patterns do not
include seam allowances.
Add ¼" seam allowance
for needle-turn appliqué.

4
Star
Make 9.

3
Center circle
Make 1.

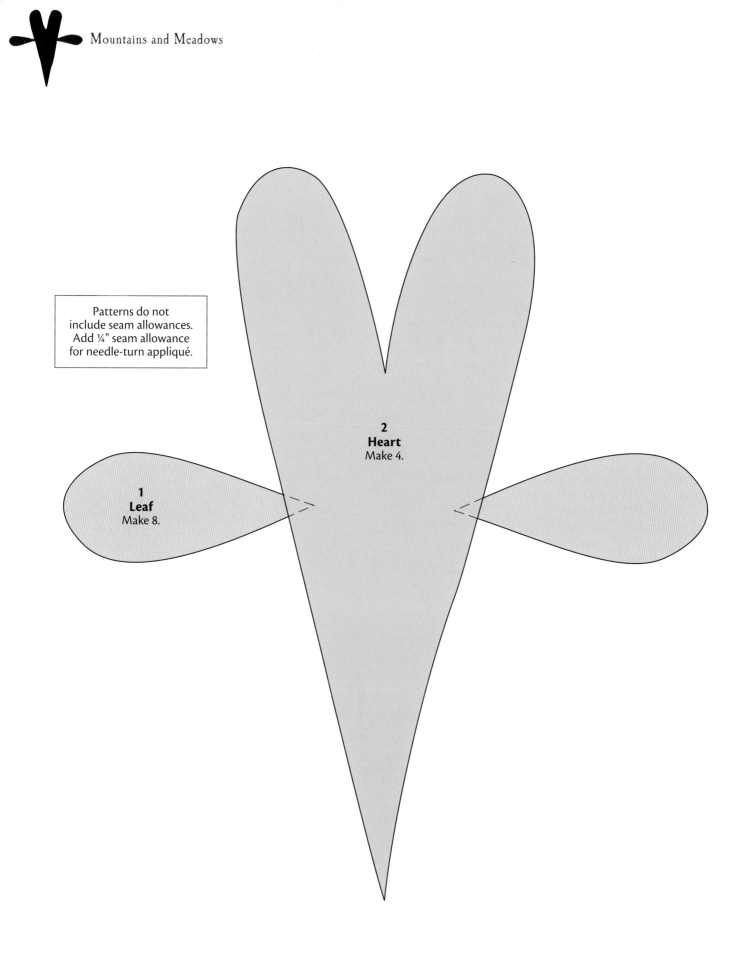

Patterns do not
include seam allowances.
Add ¼" seam allowance
for needle-turn appliqué.

2
Heart
Make 4.

1
Leaf
Make 8.

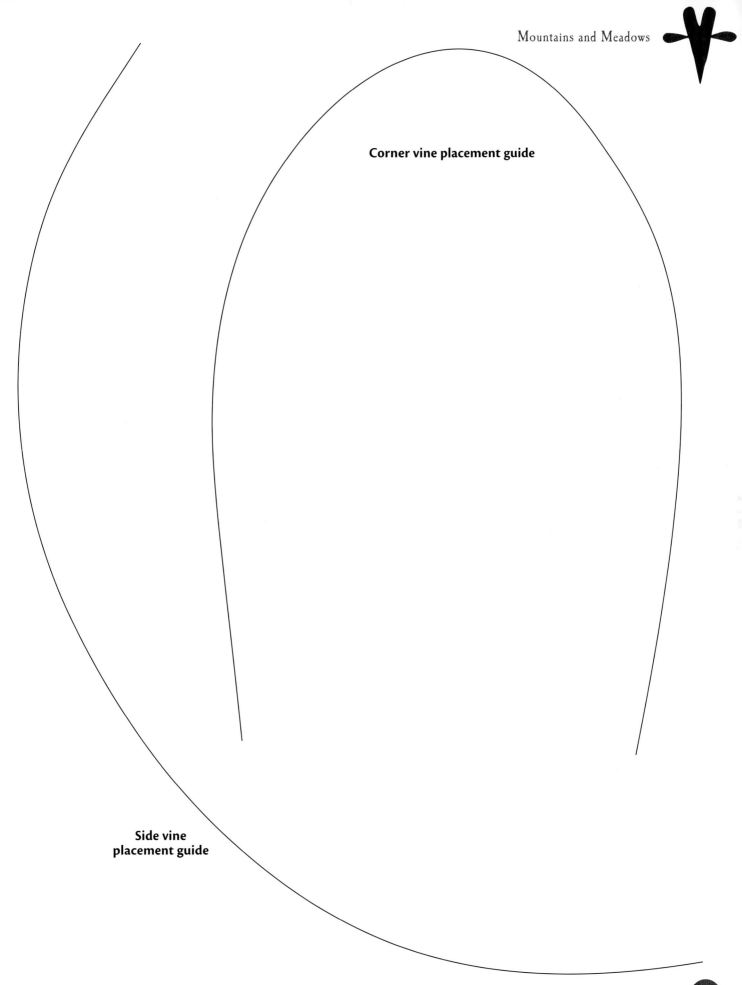

Corner vine placement guide

**Side vine
placement guide**

CHOCOLATE-COVERED CHURN DASHES

Sometimes I like to challenge myself to use fabrics that are not my usual choices. That was the case with this design. I typically don't use pink fabrics but I loved the old-fashioned look of these prints. Combining them with brown fabrics reminded me of a box of cherry-filled chocolates. Chocolate and quilting—two of my favorite things!

Hints

- As you're sewing the individual blocks, try to press the seam allowances toward the darker fabrics in each block whenever possible.

- Because the blocks are rotated when laying them out, I found it easier to wait until the blocks were stitched together into rows to press the seam allowances. Then I pressed the seam allowances in the first row in one direction. When joining the first and second rows, I made sure the seam allowances in the second row were going in the opposite direction of those in the first row so that they butted against each other. After sewing the rows together, I then pressed the seam allowances in the same direction as they were stitched. I continued in this manner until all of the rows were joined and pressed.

Materials

Yardage is based on 42"-wide fabric.

1 yard *total* of assorted pink fabrics for blocks

1 yard *total* of assorted brown fabrics for blocks and border

⅞ yard of floral fabric for borders

⅝ yard *total* of assorted cream fabrics for blocks

½ yard of binding fabric

3 yards of backing fabric

51" x 51" piece of batting

Cutting

From the assorted pink fabrics, cut a *total* of:
- 116 squares, 2½" x 2½"
- 116 rectangles, 1½" x 2½"

From the assorted cream fabrics, cut a *total* of:
- 60 squares, 2½" x 2½"
- 48 rectangles, 1½" x 2½"
- 24 squares, 1½" x 1½"

From the assorted brown fabrics, cut a *total* of:
- 4 strips, 2½" x 30½"
- 65 squares, 2½" x 2½"
- 60 rectangles, 1½" x 2½"
- 24 squares, 1½" x 1½"

From the floral fabric, cut:
- 8 strips, 2½" x 30½"
- 20 squares, 2½" x 2½"
- 8 rectangles, 1½" x 2½"

From the binding fabric, cut:
- 5 strips, 2¼" x 42"

Piecing the Quilt Top

Refer to "Making Half-Square-Triangle Units" and "Making Flying-Geese Units" on page 8 for detailed instructions as needed.

Block 1

1. Pair four 2½" pink squares with four 2½" cream squares; sew the pairs together to make four pink/cream half-square-triangle units.

Designed and pieced by Cheryl Wall. Machine quilted by Jeanne Preto.

Finished quilt: 42½" x 42½"

Finished block: 6" x 6"

❷ Sew a brown rectangle and a pink rectangle together lengthwise. Press the seam allowance toward the brown rectangle. Make four rectangle units.

❸ Lay out one 2½" brown square, the half-square-triangle units, and the rectangle units in three rows as shown. Sew the pieces together in rows, and then sew the rows together to complete the block. Do not press the seam allowances yet (see "Hints" on page 30). Make one block.

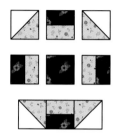

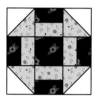

Block 1.
Make 1.

Block 2

❶ Pair two 2½" brown squares with two 2½" pink squares; sew the pairs together to make two brown/pink half-square-triangle units. Pair two 2½" cream squares with two 2½" pink squares to make two cream/pink half-square-triangle units.

❷ Make one flying-geese unit using one 1½" x 2½" brown rectangle and two 1½" cream squares. Sew the unit to a pink rectangle as shown in the block diagram.

❸ Sew a cream rectangle and a pink rectangle together lengthwise. Press the seam allowance toward the pink rectangle. Make three.

❹ Lay out one 2½" cream square and the pieces from steps 1, 2, and 3 in three rows as shown. Sew the pieces together in rows, and then sew the rows together to complete the block. Do not press the seam allowances. Make a total of four blocks.

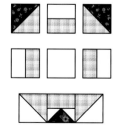

Block 2.
Make 4.

Block 3

❶ Pair two 2½" brown squares with two 2½" pink squares; sew the pairs together to make two brown/pink half-square-triangle units. Pair two 2½" cream squares with two 2½" pink squares to make two cream/pink half-square-triangle units.

❷ Sew one 1½" brown square to one end of a 1½" x 2½" cream rectangle as shown. Trim the excess fabric leaving a ¼" seam allowance and press. Repeat, sewing a brown square to one end of *another* cream rectangle as shown; press. Sew each unit to a pink rectangle as shown; press.

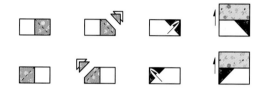

❸ Sew a brown rectangle and a pink rectangle together lengthwise. Press the seam allowance toward the brown rectangle. Make two.

❹ Lay out one 2½" brown square and the pieces from steps 1, 2, and 3 in three rows as shown. Sew the pieces together in rows, and then sew the rows together to complete the block. Do not press the seam allowances. Make a total of four blocks.

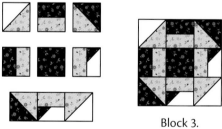

Block 3.
Make 4.

Block 4

❶ Pair two 2½" brown squares with two 2½" pink squares; sew the pairs together to make two brown/pink half-square-triangle units. Pair two 2½" cream squares with two 2½" pink squares to make two cream/pink half-square-triangle units.

❷ Make one flying-geese unit using one 1½" x 2½" cream rectangle and two 1½" brown squares. Sew the unit to a pink rectangle as shown in the block diagram. Press the seam allowances toward the pink rectangle.

③ Sew a brown rectangle and a pink rectangle together lengthwise. Press the seam allowances toward the brown rectangle. Make three.

④ Lay out one 2½" brown square and the pieces from steps 1, 2, and 3 in three rows as shown. Sew the pieces together in rows, and then sew the rows together to complete the block. Do not press the seam allowances. Make a total of four blocks.

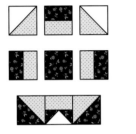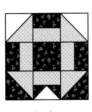

Block 4.
Make 4.

Block 5

① Pair two 2½" brown squares with two 2½" pink squares; sew the pairs together to make two brown/pink half-square-triangle units. Pair two 2½" cream squares with two 2½" pink squares to make two cream/pink half-square-triangle units.

② In the same manner as before, sew a 1½" cream square to one end of a brown rectangle as shown; trim and press. Sew a second cream square to one end of *another* brown rectangle as shown; trim and press. Sew each unit to a pink rectangle as shown; press.

③ Sew a 1½" x 2½" cream rectangle and a pink rectangle together lengthwise. Press the seam allowance toward the pink rectangle. Make two.

④ Lay out one 2½" cream square and the pieces from steps 1, 2, and 3 in three rows as shown. Sew the pieces together in rows, and then sew the rows together to complete the block. Do not

press the seam allowances. Make a total of eight blocks.

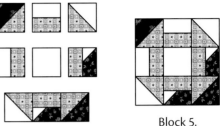

Block 5.
Make 8.

Block 6

① Pair two 2½" brown squares with two 2½" pink squares; sew the pairs together to make two brown/pink half-square-triangle units. Pair one 2½" cream square with one 2½" pink square to make one cream/pink half-square-triangle unit. Pair one 2½" floral square with one 2½" pink square to make one floral/pink half-square-triangle unit.

② In the same manner as before, sew a 1½" brown square to one end of a cream rectangle; trim and press. Sew a second brown square to one end of *another* cream rectangle as shown; trim and press. Sew each unit to a pink rectangle as shown; press.

③ Sew a brown rectangle and a pink rectangle together lengthwise. Press the seam allowance toward the brown rectangle. Make two.

④ Lay out one 2½" brown square and the pieces from steps 1, 2, and 3 in three rows as shown. Sew the pieces together in rows, and then sew the rows together to complete the block. Do not press the seam allowances. Make a total of four blocks.

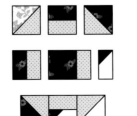

Block 6.
Make 4.

Block 7

1. Pair four 2½" floral squares with four 2½" pink squares; sew the pairs together to make four floral/pink half-square-triangle units.

2. Sew a brown rectangle and a pink rectangle together lengthwise. Sew a floral rectangle and a pink rectangle together lengthwise. Press the seam allowances toward the pink rectangles. Make two of each.

3. Lay out one 2½" brown square and the pieces from steps 1 and 2 in three rows as shown. Sew the pieces together in rows, and then sew the rows together to complete the block. Do not press the seam allowances. Make a total of four blocks. Set these blocks aside for the border.

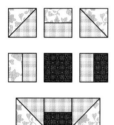
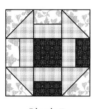

Block 7.
Make 4.

Assembling the Quilt Top

1. Arrange blocks 1–6 in five rows as shown so that the block backgrounds form the secondary Barn Raising pattern.

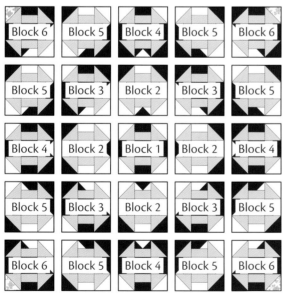

Quilt layout

2. Sew the blocks together in rows. Press the seam allowances in opposite directions from one row to the next. Then sew the rows together, pressing the seam allowances in one direction. The quilt top should measure 30½" x 30½".

Borders

1. Sew 2½"-wide floral strips to both long edges of a 2½"-wide brown strip. Press the seam allowances toward the brown strip. Repeat to make four border strips.

2. Sew a strip to the top and the bottom of the quilt top. Press the seam allowances toward the border.

3. Sew a block 7 to each end of the two remaining border strips as shown. Press the seam allowances toward the border, and then sew the borders to the sides of the quilt top, matching the seam intersections. Press the seam allowances toward the border.

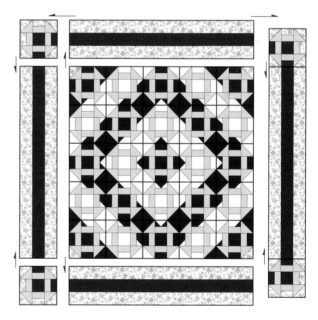

Finishing

For detailed instructions on finishing your quilt, refer to "Finishing Your Quilt" on page 10. Using the 2¼"-wide binding strips, make and attach binding.

RIBBONS AND ROSES

If you're new to quilting or working with wool, this is a great project to begin your journey. Quick and easy strip piecing and simple wool appliqué make a cozy throw, wall hanging, or table cover for your home.

Hints

- It helps to pick out the colors of the wool flowers first, and then select the coordinating cotton fabrics for the pieced blocks.

- If you want to tea dye the muslin like I did, do so before cutting the pieces. For detailed instructions, refer to "Tea Dyeing Fabric" on page 6.

Materials

Yardage is based on 42"-wide fabric.

1⅛ yards of muslin for blocks and setting triangles

⅜ yard *each* of dark green, gold, and blue fabric for blocks

¼ yard *each* of medium green, gold, and blue fabric for blocks

⅝ yard of dark blue fabric for outer border

⅜ yard of dark red fabric for inner border and corner squares

12" x 18" piece of dark green wool for stem, leaf, and bud appliqués

10" x 10" square of dark red wool for flower and bud appliqués

3" x 10" piece of dark blue wool for flower-center appliqués

3" x 10" piece of gold wool for star appliqués

½ yard of binding fabric

3¼ yards of backing fabric

55" x 55" piece of batting

Black embroidery floss

Tea for dyeing (optional)

Cutting

From *each* of the 3 dark fabrics, cut:
- 5 strips, 1½" x 42" (15 total)

From *each* of the 3 medium fabrics, cut:
- 4 strips, 1½" x 42" (12 total)

From the muslin, cut:
- 6 squares, 9½" x 9½"; cut *2 of the squares* in half diagonally to yield 4 corner triangles
- 2 squares, 14" x 14"; cut into quarters diagonally to yield 8 setting triangles

From the red inner-border fabric, cut:
- 4 strips, 1½" x 42"
- 4 squares, 3½" x 3½"

From the dark blue outer-border fabric, cut:
- 5 strips, 3½" x 42"

From the binding fabric, cut:
- 6 strips, 2¼" x 42"

Piecing the Blocks

The joy of strip piecing—sewing the fabric together in long strips, and then cutting them into squares—saves so much time in this quilt.

1️⃣ Sew three different dark strips together lengthwise to make a strip set. Press the seam allowances in one direction. Make five strip sets. From these strip sets, cut 45 segments, 3½" wide.

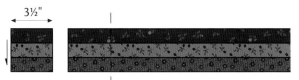

3½"

Make 5 strip sets.
Cut 45 segments.

Designed, pieced, appliquéd, and machine quilted by Cheryl Wall.
Finished quilt: 46¾" x 46¾"
Finished block: 9" x 9"

2 Sew three different medium strips together lengthwise to make a strip set. Press the seam allowances in one direction. Make four strip sets. From these strip sets, cut 36 segments, 3½" wide.

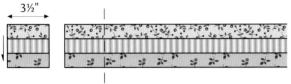

Make 4 strip sets.
Cut 36 segments.

3 Lay out five dark segments and four medium segments in three rows as shown. Sew the pieces together in rows and press the seam allowances toward the dark pieces. Sew the rows together and press. Make a total of nine blocks.

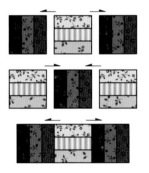 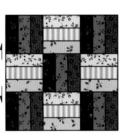

Make 9.

Assembling the Quilt Top

1 Lay out the blocks, the four muslin setting squares, and the muslin side and corner triangles in diagonal rows as shown in the photo. Sew the blocks, setting squares, and side triangles together in rows. Press the seam allowances toward the setting squares and triangles.

2 Sew the rows together, matching seam intersections. Press the seam allowances in the top rows toward the top and the seam allowances in the bottom rows toward the bottom. Add the corner triangles last and press. The setting triangles are a bit oversized. Trim and square up the quilt top, making sure to leave ¼" beyond the points of all blocks for seam allowances.

Appliqué

Refer to "Wool Appliqué" on page 9 and use the patterns on page 40.

1 From the dark green wool cut two ½"-wide strips for each of the four flowers. Cut the two strips into one 17½"-long main stem, one 7½"-long stem, and one 5"-long stem.

2 Pin the stems in place on the quilt top using the photo on page 38 as a placement guide. One end of a main stem will be placed in the corner of a block and the other end in the center of a muslin square. For each short stem, position one end of the stem underneath the main stem and the other end in the center of a muslin triangle.

3 Trace the flower, bud, and leaf shapes onto the dull paper side of the freezer paper. Cut the shapes from the wool fabrics; each flower will have two buds, one large flower, and four leaves. It's easiest to appliqué the star to the center circle, and then stitch the circle to the large oval using three strands of black embroidery floss and a blanket stitch. (Refer to "Embroidery Stitches" on page 10 as needed.) Pin the flowers and remaining shapes to the quilt top, overlapping the flowers and the buds at the ends of the stems and appliqué in place.

Borders

1 Sew the 1½"-wide red inner-border strips together end to end to make one long strip. Referring to "Borders" on page 10, measure the length of your quilt top; it should measure 38¾". Cut two strips to this length and sew them to the sides of the quilt top. Press the seam allowances toward the border.

2 Measure the width of the quilt top; it should measure 40¾". Cut two strips from the remaining long strip, and sew them to the top and bottom of the quilt top. Press.

3 Sew the 3½"-wide dark blue outer-border strips together end to end. From the long strip, cut four 40¾"-long strips. Sew border strips to the sides of the quilt top. Press the seam allowances toward the border.

4 Sew 3½" red squares to both ends of the two remaining outer-border strips. Press the seam allowances toward the border strips, and then sew the borders to the top and bottom of the quilt top, matching the seam intersections. Press.

Finishing

For detailed instructions on finishing your quilt, refer to "Finishing Your Quilt" on page 10. Using the 2¼"-wide binding strips, make and attach binding.

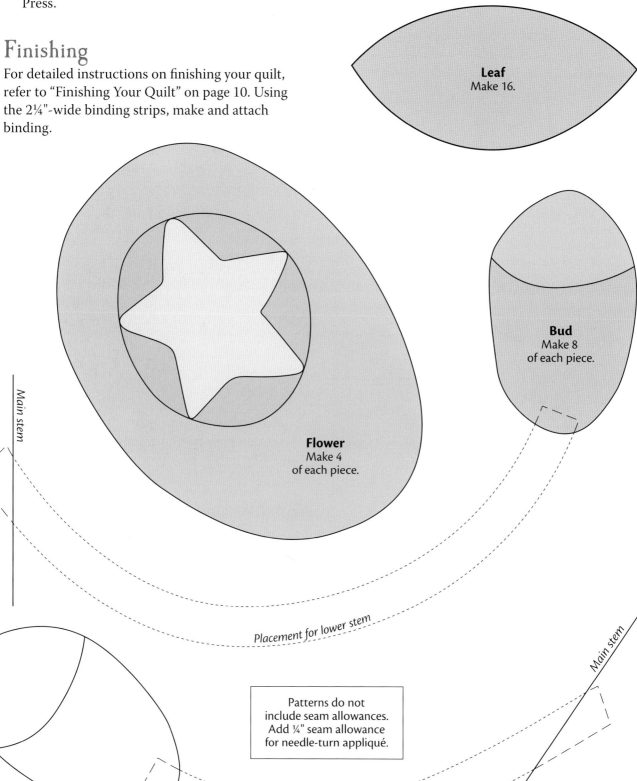

Leaf
Make 16.

Bud
Make 8
of each piece.

Flower
Make 4
of each piece.

Main stem

Placement for lower stem

Main stem

Placement for upper stem

Patterns do not
include seam allowances.
Add ¼" seam allowance
for needle-turn appliqué.

TULIP TIME

This quilt was inspired by the Trinity tulip, often found in Pennsylvania Dutch folk art. Its three petals symbolize faith, hope, and love. The initial design went through many revisions along the way and the finished quilt looks quite different from what I first envisioned—which is one of the reasons I like it!

Hint

I kept the fabrics the same within each block and used gold fabrics for all the star points. Varying the contrasting fabrics gives the quilt a scrappy, yet consistent look.

Materials

Yardage is based on 42"-wide fabric.

2¼ yards *total* of assorted medium or dark fabrics for blocks and corner squares

2 yards of muslin for blocks and border

1⅜ yards *total* of assorted gold fabrics for blocks and tulip appliqués

1⅛ yards of green fabric for stem and leaf appliqués

½ yard *total* of assorted black fabrics for blocks

½ yard of red fabric for tulip appliqués

⅝ yard of binding fabric

4¼ yards of backing fabric

72" x 72" piece of batting

Cutting

From the muslin, cut:
- 6 strips, 6½" x 42"
- 9 squares, 8½" x 8½"

From the assorted gold fabrics, cut a *total* of:
- 72 squares, 4½" x 4½"

From the assorted medium or dark fabrics, cut a *total* of:
- 20 squares, 6½" x 6½"; cut *16 of the squares* in half diagonally to yield 32 triangles
- 36 rectangles, 4½" x 8½" (you'll need 9 sets of 4 matching rectangles)
- 2 squares, 7"x 7"; cut in half diagonally to yield 4 triangles

From the assorted black fabrics, cut a *total* of:
- 22 squares, 4½" x 4½"; cut *2 of the squares* in half diagonally to yield 4 triangles

From the green fabric, cut:
- 10 strips, 1¼" x 42"

From the binding fabric cut:
- 7 strips, 2¼" x 42"

Piecing the Quilt Top

For detailed instructions, refer to "Making Flying-Geese Units" on page 8. After sewing each seam, press the seam allowances in the direction indicated by the arrows.

Whole Blocks

① Sew eight matching gold squares and four matching medium or dark rectangles together to make four flying-geese units. Repeat to make a total of 36 flying-geese units. Set aside four sets of four matching units for the quilt assembly.

2 Lay out four matching flying-geese units, four black squares, and one muslin square as shown. Sew the pieces together in rows, and then sew the rows together to complete the block. Make a total of five blocks.

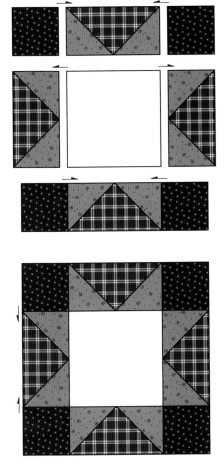

Make 5.

Filler Squares and Triangles

1 Sew the 32 medium or dark triangles together in pairs as shown to make 16 triangle pairs.

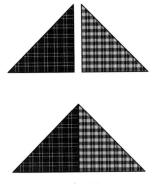

Make 16.

2 Sew two triangle pairs together as shown to make a filler square, matching the seam intersections and pressing the seam allowances in opposite directions. Make four. Set aside the remaining eight triangle pairs for the quilt assembly.

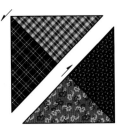

Make 4.

Assembling the Quilt Top

1 Lay out the blocks, the remaining flying-geese units, the remaining muslin squares, the triangle pairs, the filler squares, the black triangles, and the corner triangles in rows as shown. Make sure to place four matching flying-geese units around each muslin square.

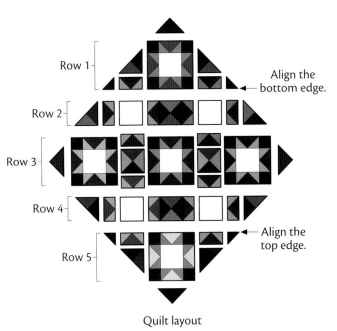

Quilt layout

Designed, pieced, and appliquéd by Cheryl Wall. Machine quilted by Jeanne Preto.
Finished quilt: 63½" x 63½"
Finished block: 16" x 16"

2 To make side triangle units, sew a black triangle and a flying-geese unit together as shown. Press the seam allowances toward the flying-geese unit. (The triangle point will jut out a bit at the top.) Then, sew a triangle pair to the flying-geese unit, keeping the side edge straight. Press the seam allowances toward the triangle pair. Make four of these units.

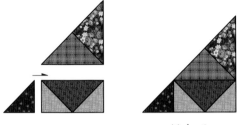

Make 4.

3 To make filler rectangles, sew flying-geese units to opposite sides of a filler square as shown. Press the seam allowances toward the filler square. Make four of these units.

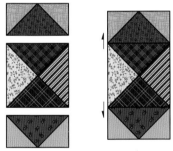

Make 4.

4 Return the units to their correct position in the quilt layout so that matching flying-geese units surround the muslin squares. Once you are satisfied with the placement, sew the pieces together in rows, keeping the edges aligned as indicated. Press the seam allowances in opposite directions from one row to the next.

5 Sew the rows together and press. Add the corner triangles last, centering each triangle along the side of the blocks. The black squares will extend beyond the edges of the quilt.

6 Using a long ruler, trim the black squares and square up the corner triangles, making sure to leave a ¼" seam allowance beyond the crossed seams all the way around the quilt top. Machine baste around the quilt top a little less than ¼"

from the outer edge to stabilize the seams, being careful not to stretch the pieces as you sew.

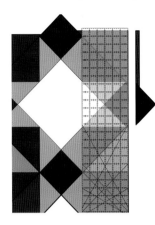

Appliqué

For detailed instructions on appliqué, refer to "Cotton Appliqué" on page 9.

1 Using the red, gold, and green fabrics and the patterns on page 46, cut out the appliqué shapes. For the blocks, you'll need 36 tulips and 36 leaves. For the border, make another 36 tulips and 72 leaves. For the stems, fold the 1¼"-wide green strips in half lengthwise, wrong sides together, and sew a scant ¼" from the raw edges. Press the seam allowances to the back of the strip. Cut 18 strips 7" long for the blocks and 36 strips 4" long for the border.

2 With a washable marker, draw two lines in the center of each muslin square as shown. Pin 7"-long stems on top of the drawn lines and appliqué them in place.

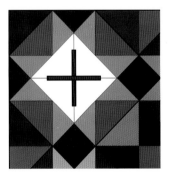

3 Pin four leaves and four tulips in the center of each muslin square as shown in the photo on page 44. Appliqué in place.

Borders

For detailed instructions on adding borders, refer to "Borders" on page 10.

❶ Sew three muslin strips together end to end to make a long strip. Make two long strips. Measure the quilt top; it should be 51½". From the long strips, cut four border strips to this length. Sew two of these strips to the top and bottom of the quilt. Press the seam allowances toward the border.

❷ Sew dark squares to both ends of the two remaining border strips. Sew these strips to the sides of the quilt, matching the seam intersections. Press the seam allowances toward the border.

❸ Using the pieced squares along the edge of the quilt center as a guide, align a ruler with the center of each square and, with a washable marker, draw vertical lines in the border strip as shown. Each border strip should have nine vertical lines to use as placement guides for the stems. Pin 4"-long stems on top of the lines and appliqué in place.

❹ Using a washable marker, place a dot 1" from the top of the stems and centered between two stems. Position the leaves so that the bottom point of the leaves meet at the stems ¼" from the raw edge of the border strip and the upper point meets at the dot and pin in place. Pin a tulip to the top of each stem. Appliqué the pieces in place. If necessary, adjust the seam allowance as you appliqué the leaves, so that the points meet at the dots between the stems.

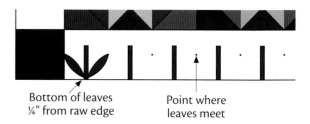

Bottom of leaves
¼" from raw edge

Point where
leaves meet

Finishing

For detailed instructions on finishing your quilt, refer to "Finishing Your Quilt" on page 10. Using the 2¼"-wide binding strips, make and attach binding.

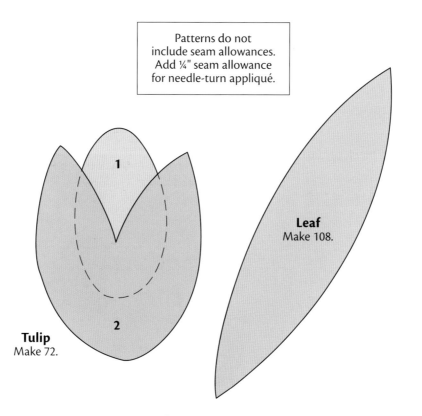

Patterns do not include seam allowances. Add ¼" seam allowance for needle-turn appliqué.

Leaf
Make 108.

1

2

Tulip
Make 72.

Bear Tracks in My Garden

When designing quilts, I'll sometimes start with a traditional block and see what happens when I break it down into smaller parts. This quilt was inspired by the Bear's Paw block. I thought the corner squares, when separated from the rest of the block, looked a bit like flowers. I also liked the design that emerged when I overlapped the blocks in the center so that they shared common points.

Hint

I used different red or rust and blue fabrics to make the Bear's Paw blocks and matching green or gold fabrics to connect the units for continuity. The light border contrasts with the dark flowers and the scrappy pieced center of this quilt, helping the flowers stand out against the background.

Materials

Yardage is based on 42"-wide fabric.

1⅝ yards of tan fabric for outer border

1 yard *total* of assorted dark red or rust fabrics for blocks and border flowers

⅞ yard *total* of assorted dark green fabrics for blocks and stem and leaf appliqués

⅔ yard *total* of assorted tan fabrics for blocks

½ yard *total* of assorted black or dark blue fabrics for blocks

⅓ yard *total* of assorted gold fabrics for the blocks

¼ yard of black fabric for inner border

½ yard of binding fabric

3¾ yards of backing fabric

64" x 64" piece of batting

Stiff paper or lightweight cardboard

Cutting

From the assorted black or dark blue fabrics, cut a *total* of:

• 81 squares, 2½" x 2½"

From the assorted tan fabrics for blocks, cut a *total* of:

• 24 rectangles, 2½" x 4½"
• 80 squares, 2½" x 2½"

From the assorted dark red or rust fabrics, cut a *total* of:

• 32 squares, 4½" x 4½"
• 28 squares, 2½" x 2½"
• 112 squares, 1½" x 1½"

From the *bias grain* of 1 dark green fabric, cut:

• 12 strips, 1¼" x 10"

From the assorted dark green fabrics, cut a *total* of:

• 24 rectangles, 2½" x 4½"
• 28 squares, 2½" x 2½"

From the assorted gold fabrics, cut a *total* of:

• 24 rectangles, 2½" x 4½"

From the black inner-border fabric, cut:

• 2 strips, 1" x 39½"
• 2 strips, 1" x 38½"

From the tan outer-border fabric, cut:

• 4 squares, 8½" x 8½"
• 24 rectangles, 3½" x 8½"
• 28 rectangles, 3½" x 4½"
• 28 rectangles, 1½" x 3½"
• 140 squares, 1½" x 1½"

From the binding fabric, cut:

• 6 strips, 2¼" x 42"

Piecing the Quilt Top

❶ Referring to "Making Half-Square-Triangle Units" on page 8, pair 72 dark blue or black squares with 2½" tan squares. Sew the pairs together to make 72 half-square-triangle units. Press the seam allowances toward the darker triangles.

❷ Sew a half-square-triangle unit to each of the eight remaining 2½" tan squares as shown. Press the seam allowances toward the squares. Make eight units.

Make 8.

❸ Sew 40 half-square-triangle units together in pairs as shown to make 20 triangle pairs. Sew the remaining half-square-triangle units together in pairs as shown to make 12 triangle pairs.

Make 20.   Make 12.

❹ Sew 2½" x 4½" tan rectangles to the triangle pairs as shown. Press the seam allowances toward the rectangles. Make 12 of each.

Make 12.   Make 12.

❺ Sew the eight remaining triangle pairs to the units from step 2 as shown and press. Make eight.

Make 8.

Assembling the Quilt Top

❶ Lay out the units, the 4½" red or rust squares, the green rectangles, the gold rectangles, and the nine remaining dark blue or black squares in rows as shown. You'll need two each of rows 1–5 and one of row 6. Sew the pieces together in rows, pressing the seam allowances in opposite directions from one row to the next.

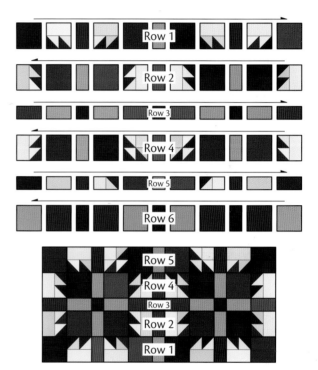

Quilt layout

❷ Sew the rows together and press the seam allowances in one direction.

❸ Sew the 38½"-long black strips to the top and bottom of the quilt top for the inner border. Sew the 39½"-long black strips to the sides of the quilt top. Press the seam allowances toward the black borders.

Border Flower Blocks

Directions in steps 1–4 are for making one flower unit. Repeat to make a total of 28 units. After sewing each seam, press the seam allowances in the direction indicated by the arrows.

Designed, pieced, and appliquéd by Cheryl Wall. Machine quilted by Jeanne Preto.
Finished Quilt: 55½" x 55½"

① Referring to "Making Half-Square-Triangle Units," pair four 1½" tan squares with four 1½" red or rust squares; sew the pairs together to make four half-square-triangle units. Press the seam allowances toward the red triangles.

② Sew two half-square-triangle units together as shown. Then sew the two remaining half-square-triangle units and a 1½" tan square together as shown.

③ In the same manner as before, sew a 2½" red square and a dark green square together to make a half-square-triangle unit. Press the seam allowance toward the green triangle.

④ Sew the units from step 2 to the half-square-triangle unit from step 3 as shown to make a flower unit. Make a total of 28 flower units.

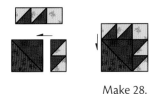

Make 28.

⑤ Sew a 1½" x 3½" tan rectangle and a 3½" x 4½" tan rectangle to each flower unit as shown. Make 16 units with flowers pointing toward the left. Make 12 units with flowers pointing toward the right.

Make 16.

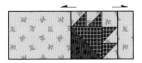

Make 12.

Appliqué

For detailed instructions, refer to "Cotton Appliqué" on page 9.

① Finger-press a crease in the center of each 3½" x 8½" tan rectangle.

② Trace the stem placement guide on page 52 onto stiff paper and cut it out to make a template. Align the straight edge on the template with the center crease on a tan rectangle. Using a washable marker, lightly trace the curved line onto 12 of the rectangles as shown. Flip the template over and trace the curved line onto the 12 remaining rectangles.

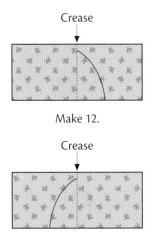

Crease

Make 12.

Crease

Make 12.

③ Fold each green bias strip in half lengthwise, wrong sides together, and sew a scant ¼" from the raw edges. Press the seam allowances to the back of the strip. Cut each strip into two 5"-long pieces. Aligning the end of the stem with the raw edge of a marked tan rectangle, place the stem along the drawn curved line, leaving the extra stem at the top of the rectangle. Pin the bottom of the stem in place and appliqué it to the rectangle, stitching about halfway on both sides, leaving the top of the stem free.

④ Lay out flower units and stem units as shown. Sew the units together, catching the bottom end of the stems in the seam line, but leaving the top end of the stems free. Press the seam allowances toward the stem units.

⑤ Finish appliquéing the stems, turning the ends under at the base of the green triangles, trimming if necessary.

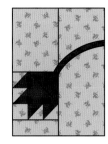

⑥ Use the leaf pattern below to make 24 green leaves. Pin and appliqué the leaves to the stems using the photo on page 50 for placement guidance as needed.

⑦ Sew two border strips to the top and bottom of the quilt top. (See the photo for the correct direction of the flowers.) Press the seam allowances toward the border.

⑧ Sew 8½" tan squares to both ends of the two remaining border strips. Press the seam allowances toward the borders and sew them to the sides of the quilt top. Press the seam allowances toward the border.

Finishing

For detailed instructions on finishing your quilt, refer to "Finishing Your Quilt" on page 10. Using the 2¼"-wide binding strips, make and attach binding.

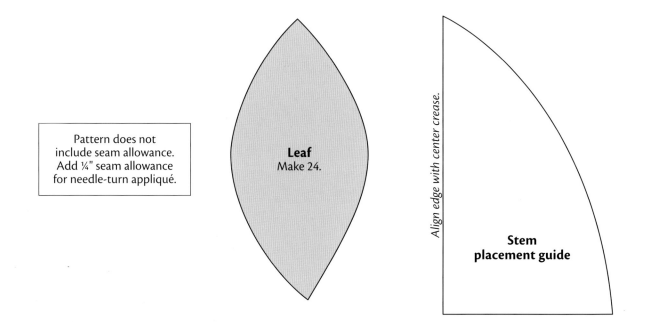

Pattern does not include seam allowance. Add ¼" seam allowance for needle-turn appliqué.

Leaf
Make 24.

Align edge with center crease.

Stem placement guide

AUTUMN EQUINOX

The fabric colors and the balance between light and dark blocks in this quilt remind me of that time of year between summer and fall, when days and nights are equally long and summer flowers are beginning to give way to autumn leaves.

Hints

- Usually, I prefer to select and cut out fabrics as I'm making a quilt, rather than doing it all ahead of time, but for this quilt I needed to know which fabrics and colors I wanted to use at least a couple of rows in advance. It's easiest to make this quilt block by block and row by row.

- If you wish to tea dye the muslin like I did, do so before cutting the individual pieces. For additional information on tea dyeing refer to page 6.

Materials

Yardage is based on 42"-wide fabric.

1½ yards of muslin for blocks and border

⅔ yard *total* of 31 assorted dark fabrics (dark blue, rust, black, and dark green) for blocks

⅔ yard *total* of 31 assorted contrasting light fabrics (gold, tan, blue, and green) for blocks

⅓ yard of green fabric for stem and leaf appliqués

¼ yard *total* of assorted red fabrics for block centers

Scraps of assorted dark blue, red, gold, and black fabrics for flower appliqués

½ yard of binding fabric

3 yards of backing fabric

50" x 58" piece of batting

Tea for dyeing (optional)

Cutting

From *each* of the 31 assorted dark fabrics, cut:
- 4 squares, 2½" x 2½" (124 total)

From *each* of the 31 assorted contrasting fabrics, cut:
- 4 squares, 2½" x 2½" (124 total)

From the assorted red fabrics, cut a *total* of:
- 31 squares, 2½" x 2½"

From the muslin, cut:
- 3 strips, 6½" x 42"
- 2 strips, 6½" x 38½"
- 4 squares, 4½" x 4½"
- 10 rectangles, 2½" x 4½"
- 46 squares, 2½" x 2½"

From the green fabric, cut:
- 2 strips, 1½" x 42"

From the binding fabric cut:
- 5 strips, 2¼" x 42"

Octagon Blocks

For each block, select four dark squares, four contrasting squares, one red square, and four background squares. Which background square you use will be determined by the octagon block you're making at the time—either two 2½" muslin squares and two contrasting squares for the blocks next to the border *or* contrasting squares from the octagon blocks in the adjacent rows. This is why you need to plan ahead!

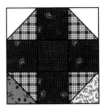

1. Lay out the four dark squares, four contrasting squares, and one red square as shown.

2. Referring to "Making Half-Square-Triangle Units" on page 8, pair the corner squares with a background square (either muslin or contrasting, depending on what the directions call for) and sew the pairs together to make half-square-triangle units. Press the seam allowances toward the darker triangle.

3. Sew the squares together into rows, pressing the seam allowances toward the dark squares. Then sew the rows together and press the seam allowances toward the center row.

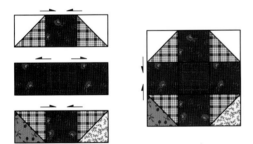

Piecing the Quilt Top

On a design wall or large flat surface, lay out the pieces for two or three rows at a time. Refer to the layout diagram on page 58 and the photo on page 56 for placement guidance as needed.

Row 1

1. Make three octagon blocks, pairing the contrasting fabric in the top corner squares with 2½" muslin squares. Pair the lower corner squares with contrasting fabric squares from the top corner squares in the next row of blocks.

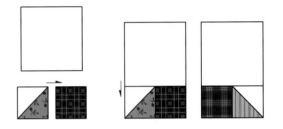

2. Make two half-square-triangle units, pairing 2½" muslin squares with contrasting fabric squares from the top corner squares in the next row of blocks. Sew a half-square-triangle unit to a dark square as shown. Press the seam allowances toward the dark square. Sew this strip to the bottom of a 4½" muslin square. Press the seam allowances toward the strip. Make one end unit and one reversed end unit.

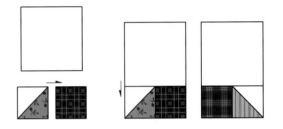

3. Select two different 2½" dark squares. Sew each square to one end of a muslin rectangle to make a sashing strip. Press the seam allowances toward the dark squares. Make two sashing strips.

4. Lay out the blocks, end units, and sashing strips as shown. Sew the pieces together to complete row 1, pressing the seam allowances away from the blocks.

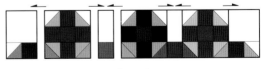

Row 1

Designed, pieced, and appliquéd by Cheryl Wall. Machine quilted by Jeanne Preto.
Finished quilt: 42½" x 50½"
Finished block: 6" x 6"

Sashing Row

Combined with the bottom squares of one row (row 1) and the top squares of the next row (row 2), the sashing row will complete a row of four blocks.

1. Select four different red squares. Select two matching dark squares from four different fabrics; the squares should also match *either* an end unit or a sashing strip in row 1. Lay out the dark squares, red squares, and three 2½" muslin squares as shown. Sew the squares together to make a sashing row. Press the seam allowances toward the dark squares.

2. Return the sashing row to your design wall, placing it below row 1. Don't sew the rows together yet!

Row 2

1. Make three octagon blocks, pairing the contrasting fabric in the top corner squares with the contrasting fabric from the sashing row to make half-square-triangle units. Pair the contrasting fabric in the bottom corner squares with the contrasting fabric from the next sashing row and make half-square-triangle units.

2. To make end units, pair contrasting squares with 2½" muslin squares to make two half-square-triangle units. Sew these to dark squares as shown and press the seam allowances toward the dark squares. Sew the strips to each side of

a muslin rectangle as shown, pressing the seam allowances toward the strips. Make one end unit and one reversed end unit.

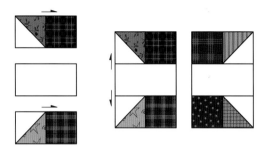

3. Sew a dark square to each side of a 2½" muslin square to make a sashing strip. Press the seam allowances toward the dark squares. Make two sashing strips.

4. Lay out the blocks, end units, and sashing strips as shown. Sew the pieces together to complete row 2, pressing the seam allowances away from the blocks.

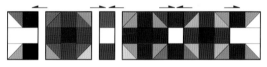

Row 2

Remaining Rows

1. Make three more sashing rows, coordinating them with the octagon blocks in the rows above and below.
2. Make two more rows similar to row 2, coordinating as before.
3. Make one additional row 1, *except* the end blocks are reversed as shown in the layout diagram.

④ Return all of the rows to your design wall, placing them in the proper order. When you're satisfied that everything is positioned correctly, sew the rows together and press the seam allowances in one direction.

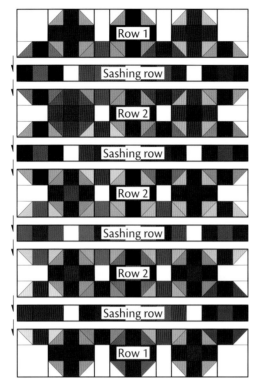

Quilt layout

Adding Borders

For detailed instructions, refer to "Borders" on page 10.

① Sew the 38½"-long muslin strips to the sides of the quilt top. Press the seam allowances toward the border.

② Sew the remaining 6½"-wide strips together end to end. Measure the width of the quilt top; it should measure 42½". Cut two strips to this length and sew them to the top and bottom of the quilt top. Press the seam allowances toward the border.

Appliqué

For detailed instructions, refer to "Cotton Appliqué" on page 9.

① In the lower-right and upper-left corners and using a washable marker, draw a 14"-long line 3" from the border seam lines as shown.

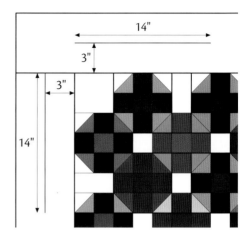

② From the green strips, cut four 1½" x 14" strips. Fold the strips in half lengthwise, wrong sides together, and sew a scant ¼" from the raw edges. Press the seam allowances to the back of the stem. Center and pin the stem on top of the line.

③ Using the assorted scraps and appliqué patterns on page 59, cut out the appliqué shapes. Make two large flowers and eight small flowers. Make six medium flowers using the two smaller shapes of the large flower and the center circle of the small flower. Make 24 leaves from the green fabric.

④ Pin the flower and leaf shapes in place using the photo on page 56 for placement guidance. A large flower should cover one end of the stem in each corner and a small flower should cover the other end of the stem. Appliqué the shapes in place.

⑤ In the same manner as before, mark 6"-long lines in the upper-right and lower-left corners. Make four 6"-long stems. Appliqué the stems in place, and then the remaining flowers and leaves.

Finishing

For detailed instructions on finishing your quilt, refer to "Finishing Your Quilt" on page 10. Using the 2¼"-wide binding strips, make and attach binding.

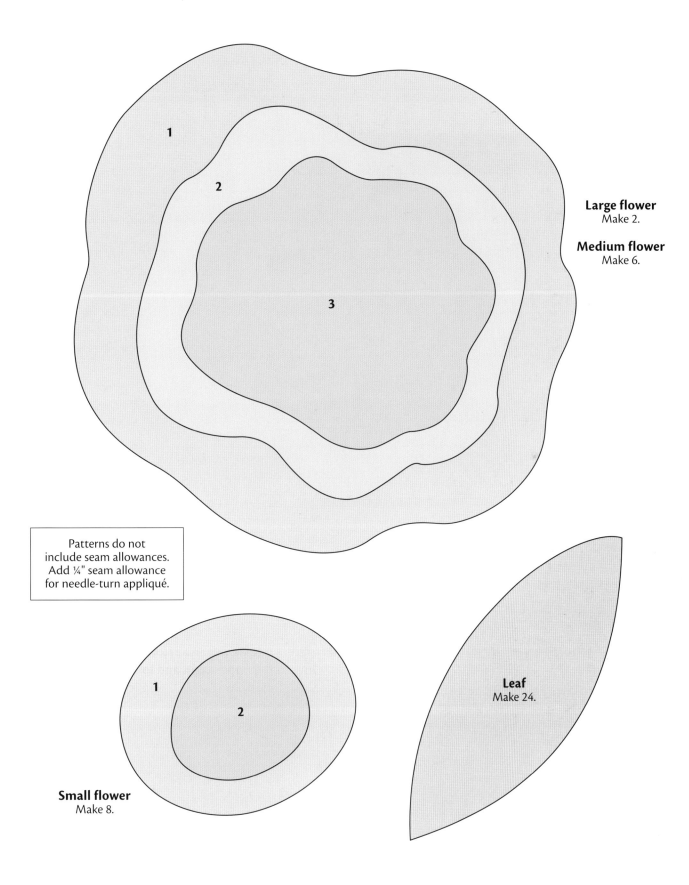

Large flower
Make 2.

Medium flower
Make 6.

Patterns do not
include seam allowances.
Add ¼" seam allowance
for needle-turn appliqué.

Leaf
Make 24.

Small flower
Make 8.

BASKETS AND BLOOMS

Crows are one of my favorite country motifs so I had
to include them in at least one quilt in this book!

Hints

- In this quilt, I used one black fabric for the Nine Patch blocks and setting triangles. In each Basket block, I used the same fabric for the handles and bases of the basket. This lends a consistency to the design, while still maintaining a scrappy look.

- Cut the bias strips for the basket handles first and use the remaining fabric for the base of the basket.

- If you wish to tea dye the muslin like I did, do so before cutting the individual pieces. For additional information on tea dyeing refer to page 6.

Materials

Yardage is based on 42"-wide fabric.

⅓ yard *each* of 9 assorted medium fabrics for baskets

⅓ yard *each* of 9 assorted dark fabrics for basket bases and handles

1½ yards *total* of assorted gold or tan fabrics for Nine Patch blocks, setting triangles, and inner border

1¼ yards of muslin for Basket block backgrounds

1⅛ yards of black fabric for Nine Patch blocks, setting triangles, and outer border

⅓ yard *total* of assorted red fabrics for Nine Patch blocks and setting triangles

¼ yard *total* of assorted dark green fabrics for stem and leaf appliqués

Scraps of assorted coordinating fabrics for flower appliqués

Scrap of black solid fabric for crow appliqués

⅝ yard of binding fabric

4 yards of backing fabric

67" x 67" piece of batting

Tea for dyeing (optional)

Lightweight cardboard or template plastic

Cutting

From *each* of the assorted medium fabrics, cut:

- 1 square, 8½" x 8½" (9 total)

From *each* of the assorted dark fabrics, cut:

- 1 bias strip, 1" x 12" (9 total)
- 3 squares, 2½" x 2½" (27 total)

From the muslin, cut:

- 5 squares, 10⅞" x 10⅞"; cut in half diagonally to yield 10 triangles
- 9 squares, 4½" x 4½"
- 18 rectangles, 2½" x 6½"

From the black fabric, cut:

- 6 border strips, 2½" x 42"
- 28 squares, 2⅞" x 2⅞"; cut in half diagonally to yield 56 triangles
- 56 squares, 2½" x 2½"

From the assorted red fabrics, cut a *total* of:

- 36 squares, 2½" x 2½"

From the assorted gold or tan fabrics, cut a *total* of:

- 13 to 14 strips, 6½" x varying lengths
- 36 rectangles, 2½" x 6½"

From *1* of the assorted dark green fabrics, cut:

- 3 strips, 1¼" x 42"; crosscut into 4 strips, 1¼" x 17", and 4 strips, 1¼" x 11"

From the binding fabric, cut:

- 7 strips, 2¼" x 42"

Designed, pieced, and appliquéd by Cheryl Wall. Machine quilted by Jeanne Preto.

Finished quilt: 59" x 59"

Finished block: 10" x 10"

Piecing the Quilt Top

After making the basket blocks, you'll have one extra muslin triangle and other large fabric pieces left over. Set these aside to use in future projects.

Basket Blocks

For each block, you'll need one medium square, three matching dark squares, and one bias strip that matches the dark squares. You'll also need one muslin triangle, two muslin rectangles, and one muslin square. Directions are for making one block. Repeat to make a total of nine blocks. After sewing each seam, press the seam allowances in the direction indicated by the arrows.

❶ Place a dark square on one corner of a medium square, right sides together. Sew diagonally from corner to corner as shown to make a basket square. Trim away the corner fabric leaving a ¼" seam allowance.

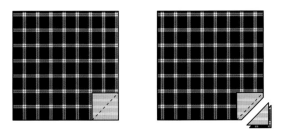

❷ Sew a dark square to one end of a muslin rectangle to make a side unit. Make two. Note: If using striped fabric for the basket base, arrange the squares as shown so the stripes are consistent.

❸ Lay out the basket square and two side units as shown. Sew the side units to the basket square,

making sure there is a ¼" seam allowance beyond the crossed seams.

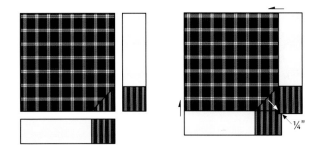

❹ With a pencil, draw a diagonal line from corner to corner on a muslin square. Pin the marked square to the corner of the basket unit from step 3, right sides together and matching the raw edges. Sew along the line and trim the excess fabric, leaving a ¼" seam allowance.

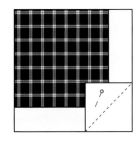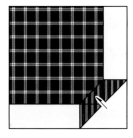

❺ Fold a muslin triangle in half and lightly crease to mark the center on the long side. Trace the handle placement guide on page 66 onto a piece of lightweight cardboard. Cut out the placement guide exactly on the line and fold it in half to mark the center on the curved edge. Matching the creased center lines and aligning the bottom edges, use a washable marker to trace a curved line onto the muslin triangle.

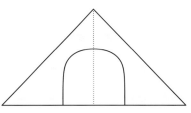

❻ Along one long edge of a dark bias strip, fold ¼" to the wrong side and press. Press the remaining long edge in the same way so that the raw edges meet in the center of the strip. The strip should be about ½" wide. Align one folded edge of the strip along the traced line on the muslin triangle. Pin and appliqué the handle in place.

7. Pin the muslin triangle to the base of the basket block, right sides together, matching the raw edges as shown (the handle will be between the two layers). Sew the pieces together using a ¼" seam allowance. Trim the basket block even with the long edge of the triangle. (Set this piece aside to use in another project.) Make a total of nine Basket blocks.

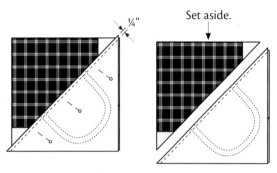

¼"

Set aside.

Trim.

Make 9.

Nine Patch Blocks

For each block, you'll need nine black squares, four red squares, and four gold or tan rectangles. Directions are for making one block. Repeat to make a total of four blocks. After sewing each seam, press the seam allowances in the direction indicated by the arrows.

1. Arrange five black and four red squares in three rows as shown. Sew the squares together in rows, and then sew the rows together to make a Nine Patch block.

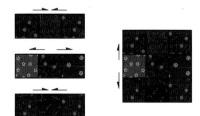

2. Sew gold or tan rectangles to the top and bottom of the Nine Patch block. Sew black squares to both ends of two gold or tan strips, and then sew the units to the center unit as shown to complete a Nine Patch block. Make a total of four blocks.

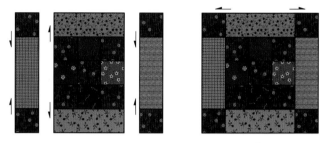

Make 4.

Side Triangles

For each side triangle, you'll need two black squares, two red squares, two gold or tan rectangles, and five black triangles. Directions are for making one side triangle. Repeat to make a total of eight triangles. After sewing each seam, press the seam allowances in the direction indicated by the arrows.

1. Sew black triangles to adjacent sides of a red square as shown, keeping the straight edges aligned. Sew a black triangle, a red square, and a black square together as shown. Then sew the two units together to make a triangle unit.

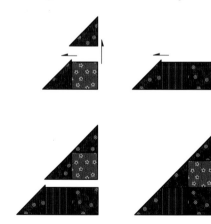

2 Sew a black triangle to one end of a gold or tan rectangle. Sew this strip to the bottom of the triangle unit from step 1 as shown.

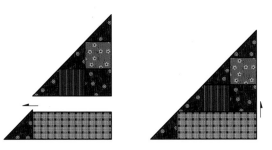

3 Sew a black square to one end of a gold or tan rectangle and a black triangle to the other end of the rectangle as shown. Sew the strip to the unit from step 2 to complete a side triangle. Make a total of eight side triangles.

Make 8.

Corner Triangles

For each corner triangle, you'll need one black square, one red square, one gold or tan rectangle, and four black triangles. Directions are for making one corner triangle. Repeat to make a total of four triangles. After sewing each seam, press the seam allowances in the direction indicated by the arrows.

1 Sew black triangles to opposite sides of a red square as shown. Sew black triangles to each end of a gold or tan rectangle as shown.

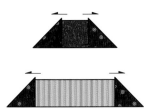

2 Center the short strip over the long strip and sew the strips together. Sew a black square to the top of the unit to complete a corner triangle. Make a total of four corner triangles.

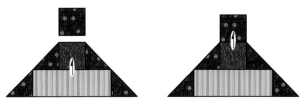

Make 4.

Assembling the Quilt Top

1 Lay out the Basket blocks, Nine Patch blocks, side triangles, and corner triangles in diagonal rows as shown. Sew the blocks and side triangles together in rows, pressing the seam allowances toward the Nine Patch blocks and side triangles.

2 Sew the rows together, matching the seam intersections and keeping the outer edges even. Center and sew the corner triangles last. Press the seam allowances in one direction. Trim and square up the corner triangles, making sure to leave ¼" beyond the crossed seams for seam allowance.

Quilt layout

Borders

For detailed instructions, refer to "Borders" on page 10.

1 Sew the 6½"-wide gold or tan strips together end to end. From the strip, cut two 43"-long strips and two 55"-long strips. Sew the shorter strips to the top and bottom of the quilt top, and then sew the longer strips to the sides of the quilt. Press the seam allowances toward the borders.

2 Sew the 2½"-wide black strips together end to end. From the strip, cut two 55"-long strips and two 59"-long strips. In the same manner as before, sew the strips to the quilt top, pressing the seam allowances toward the black strips.

Appliqué

For detailed instructions, refer to "Cotton Appliqué" on page 9.

1 Cut out the appliqué shapes, using patterns on page 67 and the assorted scraps to make four large flower circles, 12 medium flower circles, and 12 small flower circles. From the dark green, make 12 small and four large leaves. Make four black crows.

2 Along one long edge of a dark green strip, fold ¼" to the wrong side and press. Fold and press the remaining long edge in the same way to make a ¾"-wide stem. Make four short stems (11" long) and four long stems (17" long).

3 Referring to the photo on page 62 for placement guidance, place one long stem and one short stem in each corner on the gold or tan border so that the ends meet in the corner. Alternate the long and short strips on each side. Pin and appliqué in place.

4 In each corner, pin a crow on top of the stem ends. Combining the flower circles as shown in the photo, pin the flower circles and leaves over the stems and appliqué in place.

Finishing

For detailed instructions on finishing your quilt, refer to "Finishing Your Quilt" on page 10. Using the 2¼"-wide binding strips, make and attach binding.

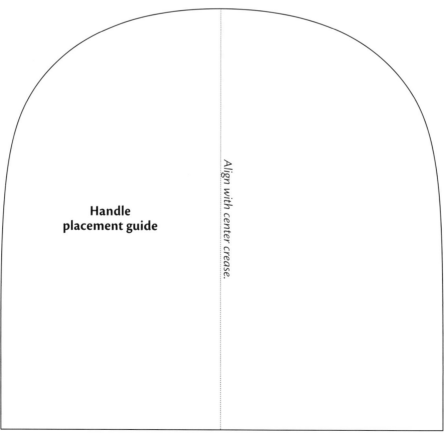

Handle placement guide

Align with center crease.

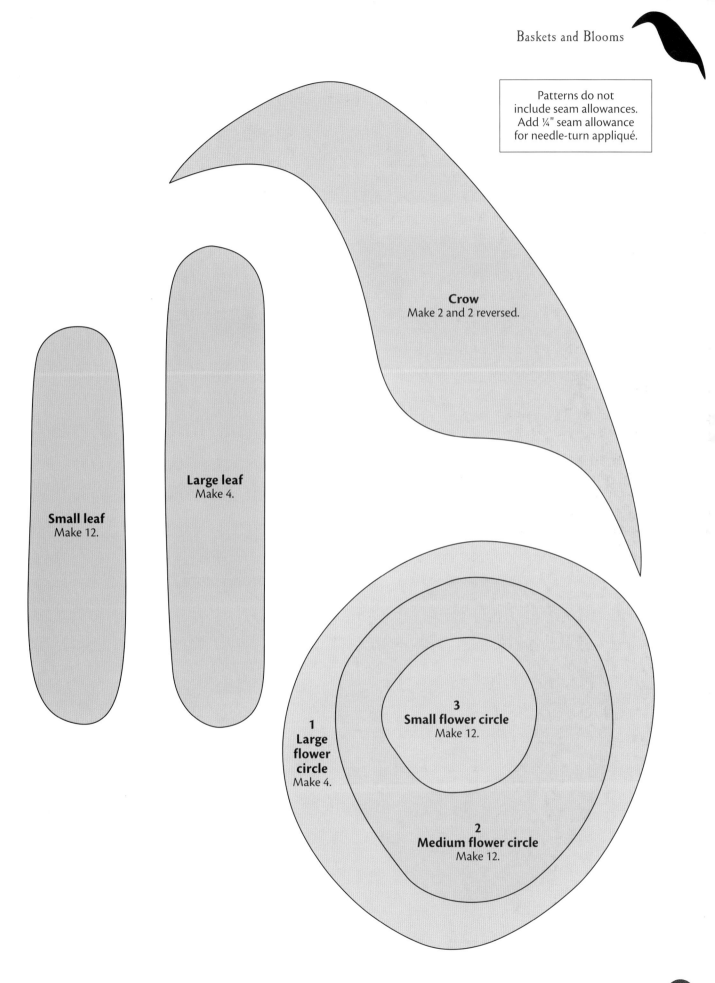

Patterns do not
include seam allowances.
Add ¼" seam allowance
for needle-turn appliqué.

Crow
Make 2 and 2 reversed.

Large leaf
Make 4.

Small leaf
Make 12.

1
Large
flower
circle
Make 4.

3
Small flower circle
Make 12.

2
Medium flower circle
Make 12.

PRAIRIE STARS

So simple and so country, this quilt reminds me of nights on the Canadian prairies, when the skies are thick with stars above the gold and brown fields of grain.

Hint

This quilt uses a variety of blue scraps—but be careful when selecting your fabrics. Try to stay with true blues and avoid those with a green or purple tint. Placing the pieces on your design wall and viewing them from a distance will help you determine which blues work best together.

Materials

Yardage is based on 42"-wide fabric.

1½ yards *total* of 16 assorted dark blue fabrics for blocks and outer border

⅞ yard *total* of 16 assorted light blue fabrics for blocks

⅞ yard *total* of 16 assorted brown fabrics for star circles

⅜ yard *total* of 16 assorted light gold fabrics for star points

⅛ yard *total* of assorted dark gold fabrics for star centers

⅓ yard of blue-and-gold print for inner border

½ yard of binding fabric

3½ yards of backing fabric

59" x 59" piece of batting

Freezer paper

Cutting

From *each* of the assorted dark blue fabrics, cut:
- 2 rectangles, 4½" x 6½" (32 total)

From the remaining assorted dark blue fabrics, cut a *total* of:
- 17 to 18 strips, 4½" x varying lengths

From *each* of the assorted light blue fabrics, cut:
- 2 rectangles, 4½" x 6½" (32 total)

From *each* of the assorted brown fabrics, cut:
- 4 squares, 2¾" x 2¾" (64 total)
- 4 rectangles, 2½" x 2¾" (64 total)

From *each* of the assorted light gold fabrics, cut:
- 4 squares, 2½" x 2½" (64 total)

From the assorted dark gold fabrics, cut a *total* of:
- 16 squares, 2½" x 2½"

From the blue-and-gold inner-border fabric, cut:
- 5 strips, 1½" x 42"

From the binding fabric, cut:
- 6 strips, 2¼" x 42"

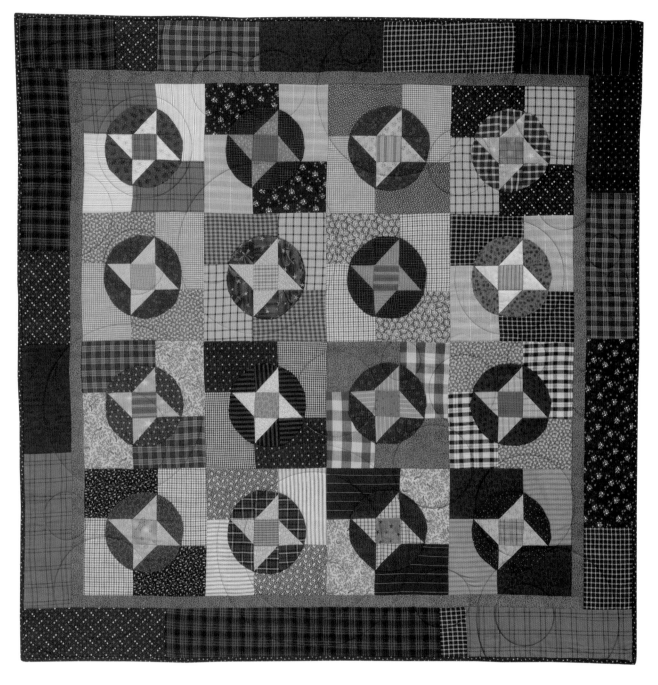

Designed, pieced, and appliquéd by Cheryl Wall. Machine quilted by Jeanne Preto.
Finished quilt: 50½" x 50½"
Finished block: 10" x 10"

Piecing the Blocks

① To make the block background, sew two matching dark blue rectangles and two matching light blue rectangles together as shown, stitching from the outer edge toward the center (there will be a hole in the center of the block). Press the seam allowances in the direction indicated by the arrows. Make 16.

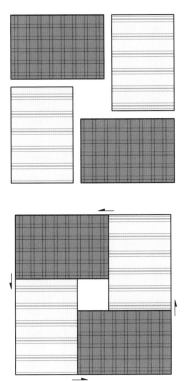

Make 16.

② To make the center star, pair four matching brown rectangles with four matching light gold squares, right sides together and matching the 2½" ends as shown. Sew diagonally across the light gold squares. Trim away the corner fabric leaving a ¼" seam allowance. Press the seam allowances toward the brown rectangles. Make four matching units for each block (64 total).

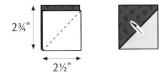

③ Lay out the units from step 2, four matching brown squares, and one dark gold square in a nine-patch arrangement as shown. Sew the pieces together in rows, and then sew the rows together to complete a center star, pressing the seam allowances away from the triangles. Make 16 center stars.

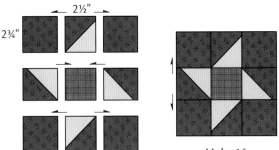

Make 16.

Appliqué

For detailed instructions, refer to "Cotton Appliqué" on page 9.

① Trace the circle on page 72 onto the dull paper side of a piece of freezer paper and cut out exactly on the line. Press the paper circle, shiny side down, onto the right side of a center star so that the star points just touch the outer edge of the circle. Cut out the star ¼" outside the paper circle. Peel off the paper and set it aside to be reused.

② Pin the star circle onto a background block, placing the center square over the hole in the block and aligning the star points with the seam lines on the background. Appliqué the circle to the background, turning the edge under ¼" as you stitch.

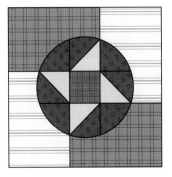

Make 16.

Assembling the Quilt Top

❶ Lay out the blocks in four rows of four blocks each, arranging the dark and light rectangles as shown. When you are satisfied with the arrangement, sew the blocks together in rows. Press the seam allowances in opposite directions from one row to the next.

❷ Sew the rows together and press the seam allowances in one direction.

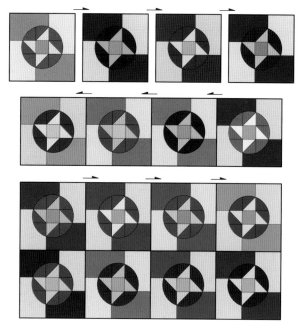

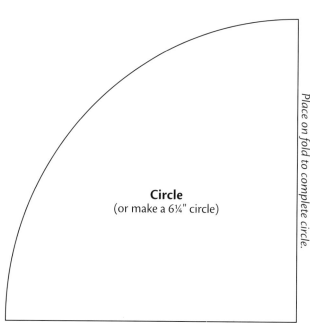

Quilt layout

Borders

For detailed instructions, refer to "Borders" on page 10.

❶ For the inner border, sew the 1½"-wide blue-and-gold strips together end to end. From the strip, cut two 40½"-long strips and two 42½"-long strips. Sew the shorter strips to the sides of the quilt top. Sew the longer strips to the top and the bottom of the quilt top. Press the seam allowances toward the border.

❷ For the outer border, sew the 4½"-wide dark blue strips together end to end. From the strip, cut two 42½"-long strips and two 50½"-long strips. In the same manner as before, sew the strips to the quilt top and press the seam allowances toward the borders.

Finishing

For detailed instructions on finishing your quilt, refer to "Finishing Your Quilt" on page 10. Using the 2¼"-wide binding strips, make and attach binding.

Circle
(or make a 6¼" circle)

Place on fold to complete circle.

Place on fold to complete circle.

Pattern does not include seam allowance. Add ¼" seam allowance for needle-turn appliqué.

GARDEN AT THE CABIN

I love designing quilts with lots of different blocks. That way,
I know I won't get bored making them! Here's my version of a
sampler quilt—Log Cabin blocks, Star blocks, and simple
appliquéd baskets, stars, hearts, and flowers. Have fun!

Hint

Cut bias strips for the vine first, and then cut the leaf appliqués from the leftover fabric.

Materials

Yardage is based on 42"-wide fabric.

2⅓ yards *total* of assorted light background fabrics for blocks and border

1¼ yards of dark fabric for borders

¼ yard *each* of 3 different medium fabrics for baskets

⅞ yard *total* of assorted dark fabrics for blocks

¾ yard of dark green fabric for vine, stem, and leaf appliqués

⅝ yard of red fabric for blocks, corner squares, and inner border

Scraps of fabric for heart, flower, and star appliqués

⅝ yard of binding fabric

4¼ yards of backing fabric

72" x 72" piece of batting

Cutting

From the red fabric, cut:
• 6 strips, 2" x 42"
• 4 squares, 3½" x 3½"
• 8 squares, 2" x 2"

From the assorted dark fabrics, cut a *total* of:
• 8 squares, 6½" x 6½"
• 4 squares, 3½" x 3½"
• 4 rectangles, 2" x 9½"
• 4 rectangles, 2" x 8"
• 4 rectangles, 2" x 6½"
• 4 rectangles, 2" x 5"
• 4 rectangles, 2" x 3½"
• 4 squares, 2" x 2"

From *each of 4* assorted dark fabrics, cut:
• 8 squares, 2" x 2" (32 total)

From the dark border fabric, cut:
• 6 strips, 3½" x 42"
• 6 strips, 2" x 33½"
• 4 sashing strips, 2" x 6½"

From the assorted light fabrics, cut a *total* of:
• 16 squares, 9½" x 9½"
• 12 squares, 6½" x 6½"
• 4 rectangles, 2" x 9½"
• 4 rectangles, 2" x 8"
• 4 rectangles, 2" x 6½"
• 4 rectangles, 2" x 5"
• 4 rectangles, 2" x 3½"
• 4 squares, 2" x 2"

From *1* of the assorted light fabrics, cut:
• 2 squares, 8" x 8"; cut in half diagonally to yield 4 triangles
• 8 rectangles, 2½" x 5½"
• 12 squares, 2½" x 2½"

From *each of 4* assorted light fabrics, cut:
• 4 squares, 2" x 2" (16 total)
• 4 rectangles, 2" x 3½" (16 total)

From basket fabric 1, cut:
• 12 squares, 2½" x 2½"

From basket fabric 2, cut:
• 20 squares, 2½" x 2½"

From basket fabric 3, cut:
• 12 squares, 2½" x 2½"
• 4 strips, 1" x 10¾"

From the dark green fabric, cut:
• 1"-wide bias strips to total 225"

From the binding fabric, cut:
• 7 strips, 2¼" x 42"

Log Cabin Blocks

1 Sew a 2" dark square to a 2" red square. Press the seam allowances toward the red square. Sew a 2" x 3½" dark rectangle to the left side and press the seam allowances toward the rectangle.

2 Sew a 2" x 3½" light rectangle to the bottom of the unit; add a 2" x 5" light rectangle to the right and a 2" x 5" dark rectangle to the top of the unit, pressing the seam allowances toward each just-added rectangle. Continue sewing in a *counterclockwise* direction around the block, adding a 2" x 6½" dark rectangle, a 2" x 6½" light rectangle, a 2" x 8" light rectangle, and a 2" x 8" dark rectangle. Lastly, add a 2" x 9½" dark rectangle and a 2" x 9½" light rectangle. The block should measure 9½" x 11". Make two blocks.

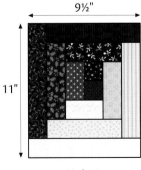

Make 2.

3 In the same manner, make two reversed blocks. Sew the first dark rectangle to the *right* of the two center squares and add rectangles in a *clockwise* direction around the block. Press the seam allowances toward the center of the block. The blocks should measure 9½" x 11".

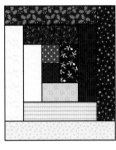

Make 2.

4 Lay out the four blocks as shown. Sew the blocks together in rows, matching the seam intersections. Press the seam allowances in opposite directions from row to row. Sew the rows together to complete the center block, pressing the seam allowances in one direction.

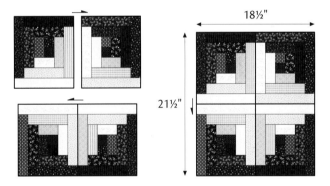

Assembling the Quilt Center

For detailed instructions, refer to "Making Half-Square-Triangle Units" on page 8.

Top and Bottom Center Borders

1 Pair a 6½" light square and a 6½" dark square, right sides together. With a pencil, draw a diagonal line on the wrong side of the light square. Sew along the line and trim the excess fabric, leaving a ¼" seam allowance. Press the seam allowances toward the dark triangle. Make a total of eight half-square-triangle units.

Designed, pieced, appliquéd, and hand quilted by Cheryl Wall.

Finished quilt: 63½" x 63½"

Finished Log Cabin blocks: 9" x 10½"

Finished Star blocks: 6" x 6"

Finished Basket blocks: 9" x 9"

2 Lay out two half-square-triangle units and one 6½" light square as shown. Sew the pieces together to make a strip, pressing the seam allowances toward the half-square-triangle units. Make four strips.

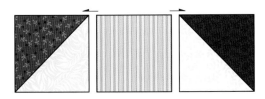

3 Sew a strip from step 2 to each short side of the center block as shown. Press the seam allowances toward the center. Sew 33½"-long dark strips to the sides of the center unit and press the seam allowances toward the strips. (Set aside the remaining two strips for the side center borders.)

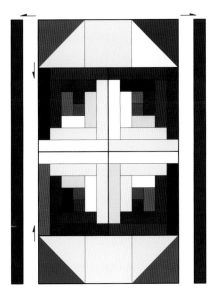

Star Blocks

For each block, you'll need four 2" light squares and four 2" x 3½" light rectangles, all matching; eight matching 2" dark squares; and one 3½" dark square for the center. Directions are for making one block. Repeat to make a total of four blocks. After sewing each seam, press the seam allowances in the direction indicated by the arrows.

1 Referring to "Making Flying-Geese Units" on page 8, use the light rectangles and the 2" dark squares to make four flying-geese units. Press the seam allowances toward the dark triangles.

2 Lay out the flying-geese units, the light squares, and the 3½" dark square as shown. Sew the pieces together in rows, and then sew the rows together to complete a Star block. Make a total of four Star blocks.

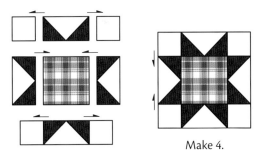

Make 4.

Side Center Border

1 Lay out two Star blocks, two 2" x 6½" dark sashing strips, and one center border strip as shown. Sew the pieces together to make a border strip, pressing the seam allowances toward the dark strips. Repeat to make a second border strip. Sew the border strips to opposite sides of the center unit as shown and press the seam allowances toward the dark strips.

2 Sew 33½"-long dark strips to the sides of the center unit. Press the seam allowances toward the dark strips.

③ Sew 2" red squares to each end of the two remaining 33½"-long dark strips. Sew these strips to the top and bottom of the center unit, matching the seam intersections. Press.

Basket Blocks

For each block, you'll need three 2½" basket fabric 1 squares, five 2½" basket fabric 2 squares, three 2½" basket fabric 3 squares, one 1" x 10¾" basket 3 strip, two 2½" x 5½" light rectangles, three 2½" light squares, and one 8" light triangle. Directions are for making one block. Repeat to make a total of four blocks. After sewing each seam, press the seam allowances in the direction indicated by the arrows.

① Refer to "Making Half-Square-Triangle Units" on page 8 to make the following:

- two half-square-triangle units, pairing basket fabric 1 and basket fabric 2 squares
- one half-square-triangle unit, pairing basket fabric 1 and basket fabric 3 squares
- two half-square-triangle units, pairing basket fabric 3 and two light squares

② Lay out the three half-square-triangle units using basket fabric 1 and the three remaining basket fabric 2 squares as shown. Sew the pieces together in rows, and then sew the rows

together. Trim away the excess fabric, leaving a ¼" seam allowance beyond the crossed seams.

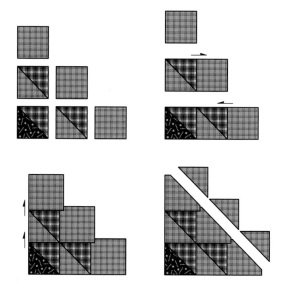

③ Center and sew a 1" x 10¾" basket fabric 3 strip to the long edge of the basket unit from step 2; the strip ends will extend beyond the triangle as shown. Trim the strip even with the edges of the basket unit.

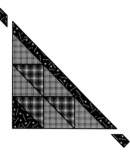

④ Sew one basket fabric 3/light half-square-triangle unit to one end of a light rectangle to make a side unit. Sew the remaining basket fabric 3/ light half-square-triangle unit, a light rectangle, and a light square together as shown to make a second side unit.

5 Lay out the basket unit from step 3 and the two side units from step 4. Sew the units together to complete the basket unit.

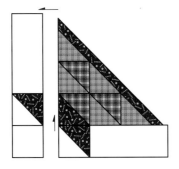

6 Center and sew the long side of a light triangle to the long side of the basket unit to complete a basket block. Make a total of four basket blocks.

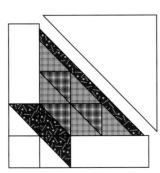

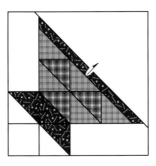

Make 4.

Appliqué

For detailed instructions, refer to "Cotton Appliqué" on page 9. Refer to the photo on page 76 for placement guidance as needed.

1 Sew four 9½" light squares together to make a border strip. Make four strips. Sew a border strip to the top and bottom of the quilt top and press.

2 Sew a basket block to both ends of the two remaining strips as shown; press. Sew the strips to the sides of the quilt top, matching the seam intersections. Press the seam allowances toward the dark border.

Quilt layout

3 Sew the dark green bias strips together end to end to make one long strip. For the stems, cut four 8½"-long strips and four 12½"-long strips. Cut the remaining strip into four equal pieces for the vines. On one long edge of each strip, fold and press a generous ¼" to the wrong side. Press the remaining long edge in the same way so that the raw edges overlap. The vines should be about ⅜" wide. Fold and press the stems in the same manner.

4 Pin the vines to the light border, leaving 1" of vine overlapping the basket rims in each corner. Turn under the vine ends 1", aligning them with the basket rims, and appliqué the vine in place.

5 Using the assorted scraps, the dark green fabric, and the patterns on pages 80–83, cut out the appliqué shapes. Make the quantity indicated on the pattern for each shape. On each side, pin two flowers, one star, and six leaves to the vine and appliqué in place. For border flower 3, cut out a circle for shape 1, and then appliqué shape 2 to the circle. Appliqué the center circle (shape 3) on top of shape 2, and then appliqué the flower to the vine.

⑥ Pin and appliqué the prepared stems to the quilt center. Pin and appliqué the remaining large flower, small flowers, buds, and center leaves to the stems. Appliqué the hearts and heart leaves to the center border.

Borders

For detailed instructions, refer to "Borders" on page 10.

① Sew the 2"-wide red strips together end to end. From the long strip, cut four 54½"-long strips. Sew two strips to the top and bottom of the quilt, pressing the seam allowances toward the red border.

② Sew 2" light squares to both ends of the two remaining strips. Sew the strips to the sides of the quilt and press the seam allowances toward the red border.

③ Sew the 3½"-wide dark strips together end to end. From the long strip, cut four 57½"-long strips. Sew two strips to the top and bottom of the quilt. Sew 3½" red squares to both ends of the two remaining strips and sew them to the sides of the quilt. Press the seam allowances toward the dark borders.

Finishing

For detailed instructions on finishing your quilt, refer to "Finishing Your Quilt" on page 10. Using the 2¼"-wide binding strips, make and attach binding.

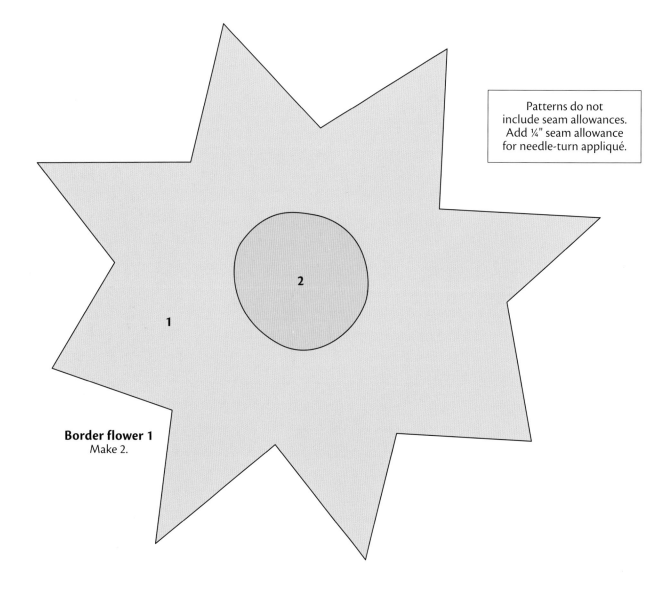

Patterns do not include seam allowances. Add ¼" seam allowance for needle-turn appliqué.

Border flower 1
Make 2.

Patterns do not include seam allowances. Add ¼" seam allowance for needle-turn appliqué.

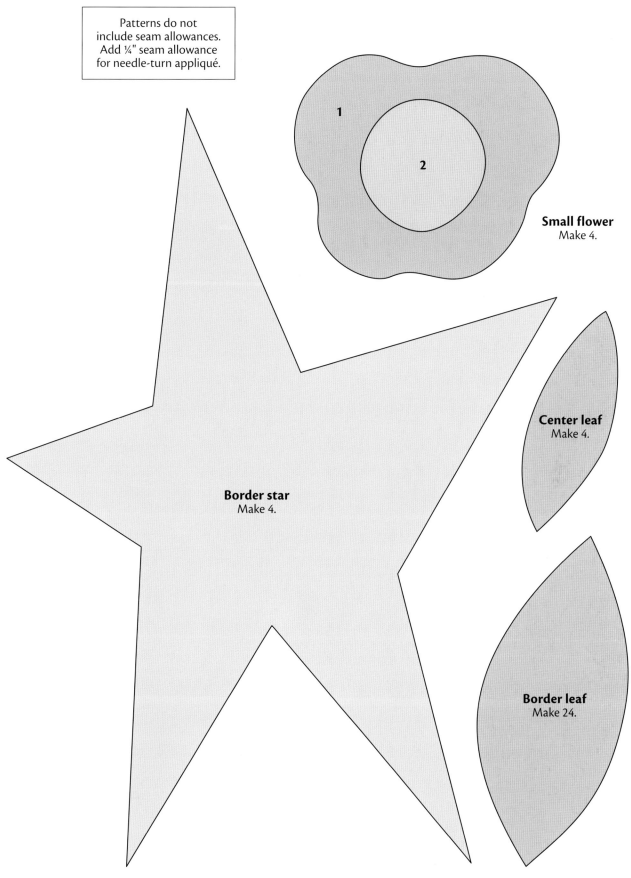

1

2

Small flower
Make 4.

Center leaf
Make 4.

Border star
Make 4.

Border leaf
Make 24.

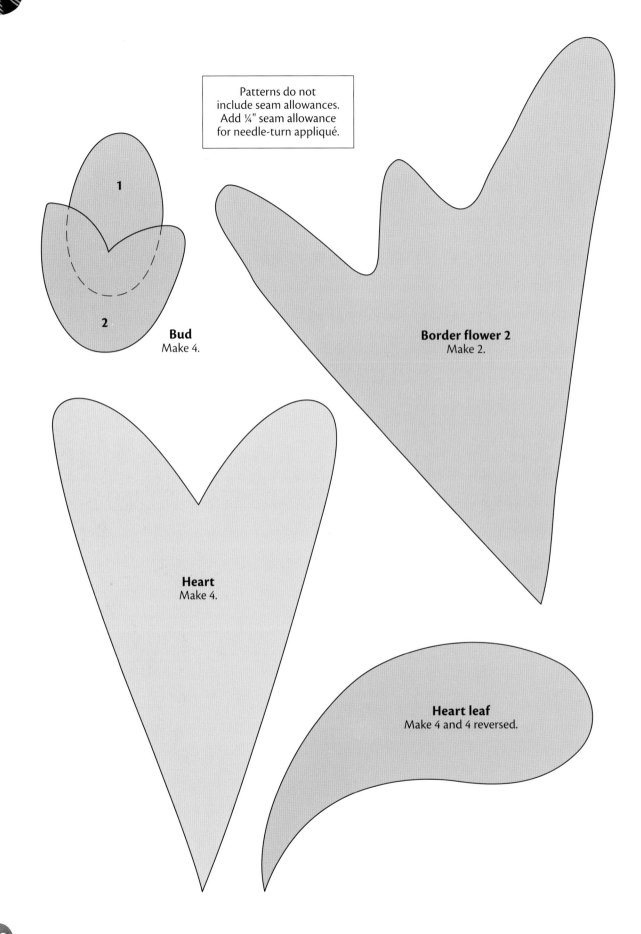

Patterns do not include seam allowances. Add ¼" seam allowance for needle-turn appliqué.

1

2

Bud
Make 4.

Border flower 2
Make 2.

Heart
Make 4.

Heart leaf
Make 4 and 4 reversed.

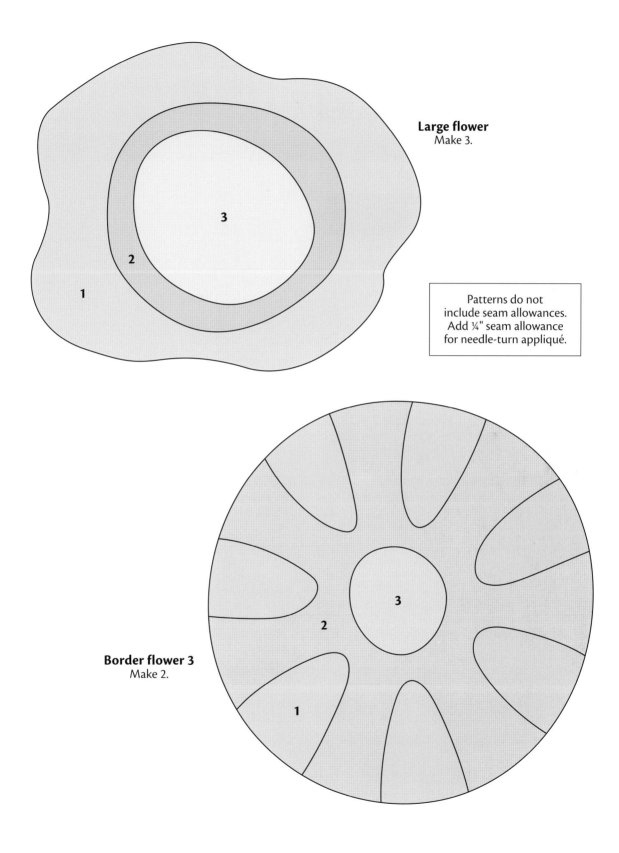

Large flower
Make 3.

3

2

1

Patterns do not
include seam allowances.
Add ¼" seam allowance
for needle-turn appliqué.

Border flower 3
Make 2.

3

2

1

Over, Under, Around, and Through

I love using lots of different fabrics in my quilts, but sometimes I challenge myself to limit the number of fabrics I can use in one design. For this quilt, I chose only four fabrics to produce a woven Churn Dash border around a checkered center.

Hint

I used the same dark fabric for the blocks, inner border, and binding. If you prefer to use a different fabric for the binding, you'll need 1 yard of dark fabric for the blocks and inner border and ½ yard of fabric for the binding.

Materials

Yardage is based on 42"-wide fabric.

2¼ yards of light fabric for blocks and outer border

1½ yards of medium fabric for blocks

1⅓ yards of dark fabric for blocks, inner border, and binding

⅓ yard of red fabric for blocks and corner squares

3¾ yards of backing fabric

64" x 64" piece of batting

Cutting

From the dark fabric, cut:
- 6 binding strips, 2¼" x 42"
- 7 strips, 1½" x 42"
- 2 strips, 4½" x 14"
- 4 strips, 1½" x 13"
- 50 rectangles, 1½" x 4½"

From the medium fabric, cut:
- 2 strips, 2½" x 42"
- 6 strips, 1½" x 42"
- 20 squares, 4½" x 4½"
- 32 squares, 3½" x 3½"
- 32 squares, 2½" x 2½"
- 16 rectangles, 1½" x 3½"

From the light fabric, cut:
- 5 strips, 4½" x 42"
- 2 strips, 2½" x 42"
- 6 strips, 1½" x 42"
- 16 squares, 4½" x 4½"
- 32 squares, 3½" x 3½"
- 32 squares, 2½" x 2½"
- 16 rectangles, 1½" x 3½"

From the red fabric, cut:
- 4 squares, 4½" x 4½"
- 1 strip, 1½" x 14"
- 2 strips, 1½" x 13"
- 4 squares, 1½" x 1½"

Piecing the Blocks

This quilt is made using four different block variations. The two different center blocks and the two different Churn Dash blocks are essentially the same, but color placement creates the checkered design and the woven border. After sewing each seam, press the seam allowances in the direction indicated by the arrows.

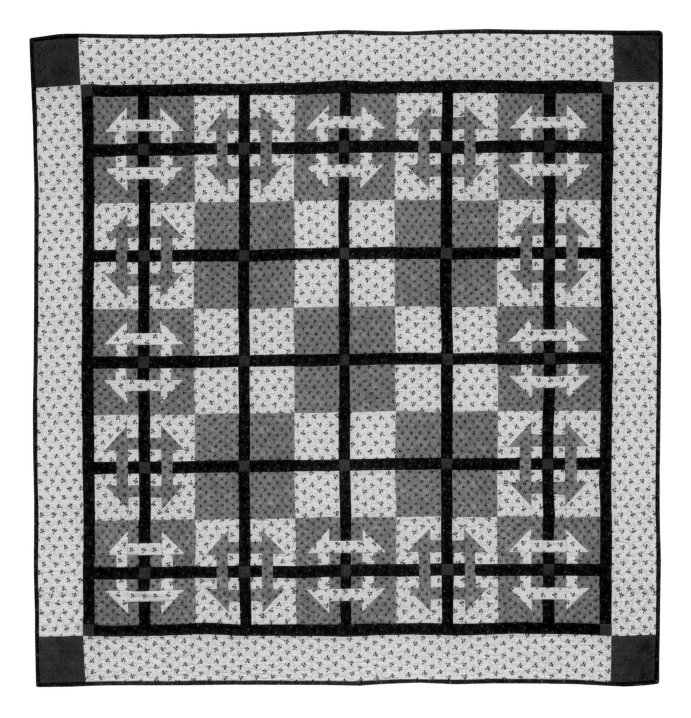

Designed, pieced, and machine quilted by Cheryl Wall.
Finished quilt: 55½" x 55½"
Finished block: 9" x 9"

Block 1

① Place a 2½" light square on one corner of a 3½" medium square, right sides together. Sew diagonally from corner to corner as shown. Trim away the corner fabric leaving a ¼" seam allowance. Make 32.

Make 32.

② Sew two 1½" x 42" medium strips and one 1½" x 42" dark strip together lengthwise as shown to make a strip set. Crosscut the strip set into 16 segments, 2½" wide.

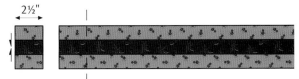

Cut 16 segments.

③ Sew a 1½" x 3½" light rectangle to each segment from step 2 as shown. Make 16.

Make 16.

④ Sew a unit from step 3 between two squares from step 1 as shown. Make 16 units.

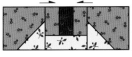

Make 16.

⑤ Sew one 2½" x 42" medium strip, one 1½" x 42" light strip, and one 1½" x 42" medium strip together lengthwise as shown to make a strip set. Make two of these strip sets. Crosscut the strip sets into 32 segments, 1½" wide.

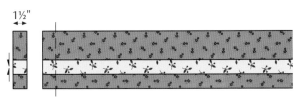

Make 2 strip sets.
Cut 32 segments.

⑥ Sew a 1½" x 4½" dark rectangle between two segments from step 5 as shown. Make 16.

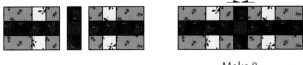

Make 16.

⑦ Sew two 1½" x 13" dark strips and one 1½" x 13" red strip together lengthwise as shown to make a strip set. Crosscut the strip set into eight segments, 1½" wide.

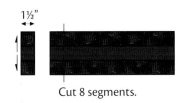

Cut 8 segments.

⑧ Sew one segment from step 7 between two units from step 6 to make a center unit. Make eight.

Make 8.

⑨ Sew a center unit between two units from step 4 to complete block 1. Make a total of eight blocks.

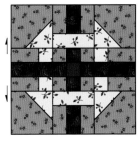

Block 1.
Make 8.

Block 2

1. Referring to step 1 of "Block 1" on page 87, sew a 2½" medium square to one corner of a 3½" light square. Make 32.

2. Sew two 1½" x 42" light strips and one 1½" x 42" dark strip together lengthwise as shown to make a strip set. Crosscut the strip set into 16 segments, 2½" wide.

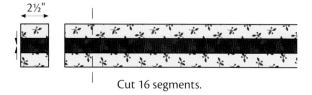

Cut 16 segments.

3. Sew a 1½" x 3½" medium rectangle to each segment from step 2. Make 16.

Make 16.

4. Sew a unit from step 3 between two squares from step 1 as shown. Make 16 units.

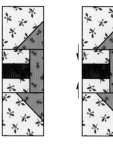

Make 16.

5. Sew one 2½" x 42" light strip, one 1½" x 42" medium strip, and one 1½" x 42" light strip together lengthwise as shown to make a strip set. Make two of these strip sets. Crosscut the strip sets into 32 segments, 1½" wide.

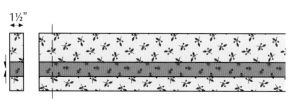

Make 2 strip sets.
Cut 32 segments.

6. Sew a 1½" x 4½" dark rectangle between two segments from step 5 as shown. Make 16.

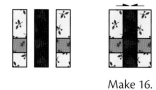

Make 16.

7. Sew two 1½" x 13" dark strips and one 1½" x 13" red strip together lengthwise as shown to make a strip set. Crosscut the strip set into eight segments, 1½" wide.

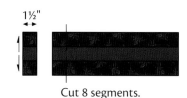

Cut 8 segments.

8. Sew one segment from step 7 between two units from step 6 to make a center unit. Make eight.

Make 8.

9. Sew a center unit between two units from step 4 to complete block 2. Press the seam allowances toward the center. Make a total of eight blocks.

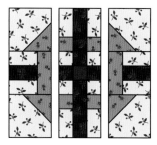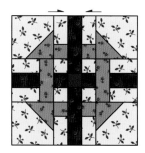

Block 2.
Make 8.

Blocks 3 and 4

① Sew two 4½" x 14" dark strips and one 1½" x 14" red strip together lengthwise as shown to make a strip set. Crosscut the strip set into nine segments, 1½" wide.

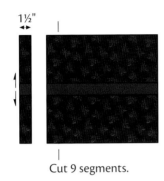

1½"

Cut 9 segments.

② Sew a 1½" x 4½" dark rectangle between two 4½" medium squares. Make two. Sew one segment from step 1 between these two units to complete block 3. Repeat to make a total of five blocks.

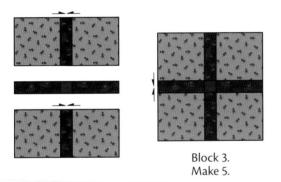

Block 3.
Make 5.

③ Sew a 1½" x 4½" dark rectangle between two 4½" light squares. Make two. Sew one segment from step 1 between these two units to complete block 4. Repeat to make a total of four blocks.

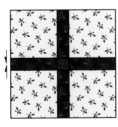

Block 4.
Make 4.

Assembling the Quilt Top

① Lay out the blocks in five rows of five blocks each as shown in the quilt layout diagram, alternating the light blocks and medium blocks and placing blocks 3 and 4 in the center.

② Sew the blocks together in rows. Press the seam allowances in opposite directions from one row to the next. Then sew the rows together and press the seam allowances in one direction.

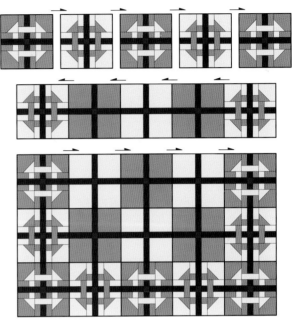

Quilt layout

Borders

For detailed instructions, refer to "Borders" on page 10.

① For the inner border, sew the remaining 1½"-wide dark strips together end to end. From the strip, cut four 45½"-long strips. Sew a strip to the top and bottom of the quilt top. Sew 1½" red squares to both ends of the two remaining dark strips. Sew these strips to the sides of the quilt top, pressing the seam allowances toward the border.

② For the outer border, sew the 4½"-wide light strips together end to end. From the strip, cut four 47½"-long strips. Sew a strip to the top and bottom of the quilt top. Sew 4½" red squares to both ends of the two remaining light strips and sew the strips to the sides of the quilt top. Press the seam allowances toward the border.

Finishing

For detailed instructions on finishing your quilt, refer to "Finishing Your Quilt" on page 10. Using the 2¼"-wide binding strips, make and attach binding.

FLOWERS IN THE SNOW

Typically I don't design quilts with white fabric, but I used white in this quilt to achieve the effect of the snow. The rich reds and greens of the roses contrast beautifully with the white-and-cream background.

Hint

One way to choose fabrics for a quilt is to start with a favorite multicolored print as the predominant fabric. Then, select other fabrics that complement the main print and use these as accents. For this quilt, I chose the rose print first, and then added the green, red, gold, and cream fabrics to echo the colors found in the rose print.

Materials

Yardage is based on 42"-wide fabric.

2½ yards of floral fabric for blocks and outer border

1½ yards *total* of assorted dark fabrics for blocks

1⅜ yards *total* of assorted light fabrics for blocks

½ yard of dark fabric for inner border

⅓ yard of dark fabric for middle border

⅝ yard of binding fabric

4⅜ yards of backing fabric

74" x 74" piece of batting

Cutting

From the assorted light fabrics for blocks, cut a *total* of:

• 276 squares, 2½" x 2½"

From the assorted dark fabrics for blocks, cut a *total* of:

• 300 squares, 2½" x 2½"

From the floral fabric, cut:

• 7 strips, 4½" x 42"

• 19 strips, 2½" x 42"; crosscut into:
  - 16 rectangles, 2½" x 12½"
  - 16 rectangles, 2½" x 10½"
  - 13 rectangles, 2½" x 8½"
  - 18 rectangles, 2½" x 6½"
  - 9 rectangles, 2½" x 4½"

From the dark inner-border fabric, cut:

• 6 strips, 2½" x 42"

From the dark middle-border fabric, cut:

• 6 strips, 1½" x 42"

From the binding fabric, cut:

• 7 strips, 2¼" x 42"

Piecing the Quilt Top

For detailed instructions, refer to "Making Half-Square-Triangle Units" on page 8. Directions are for making one of each block. Repeat to make the number of blocks indicated. After sewing each seam, press the seam allowances in the direction indicated by the arrows.

Block 1

1. Sew light and dark squares together in pairs to make 12 half-square-triangle units. Press the seam allowances toward the dark triangles.

2. Arrange two half-square-triangle units and two dark squares as shown. Sew the squares together in rows, and then sew the rows together.

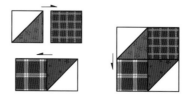

Designed and pieced by Cheryl Wall. Machine quilted by Jeanne Preto.

Finished quilt: 65½" x 65½"

Finished block: 12" x 12"

3 Sew a 2½" x 4½" floral rectangle to the top of the unit. Sew 2½" x 6½" floral rectangles to the left side and bottom of the unit. Then sew a 2½" x 8½" floral rectangle to the right side of the unit.

4 Lay out the remaining half-square-triangle units, six dark squares, and four light squares in four rows as shown. Sew the squares in each row together.

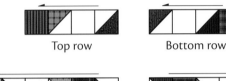

Top row   Bottom row

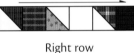

Left row   Right row

5 Sew the top and bottom rows to the center unit. Then sew the side rows to the left and right sides of the unit to complete the block. Make a total of nine blocks.

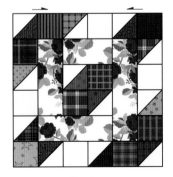

Block 1.
Make 9.

Block 2

1 Sew light and dark squares together in pairs to make eight half-square-triangle units. Press the seam allowances toward the dark triangles.

2 Lay out the half-square-triangle units, four dark squares, and four light squares in four rows as shown. Sew the squares together in rows. Then sew the rows together.

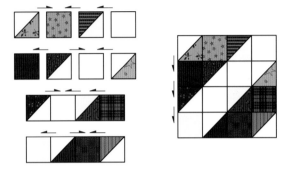

3 Sew a 2½" x 8½" floral rectangle to the top of the center unit. Sew 2½" x 10½" floral rectangles to the left side and bottom of the unit. Then sew a 2½" x 12½" floral rectangle to the right side of the unit to complete the block. Make a total of four blocks.

Block 2.
Make 4.

Half Block 1

1 Sew light and dark squares together in pairs to make four half-square-triangle units. Press the seam allowances toward the dark triangles. Lay out the half-square-triangle units, two dark squares, and four light squares in four rows as shown. Sew the squares together in rows. Then sew the rows together.

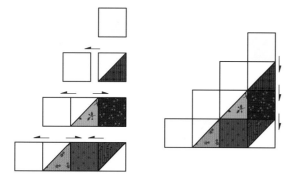

2 Sew a 2½" x 10½" floral rectangle to the bottom of the unit. Then sew a 2½" x 12½" floral rectangle to the right side to complete the half block. Make a total of four of half block 1.

Half-block 1.
Make 4.

Half Block 2

1 Sew light and dark squares together in pairs to make six half-square-triangle units. Press the seam allowances toward the dark triangles. Lay out the half-square-triangle units, two dark squares, and two light squares in four rows as shown. Sew the squares together in rows. Then sew the rows together.

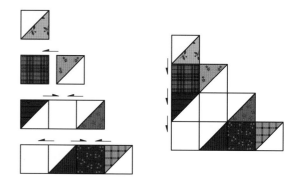

2 Sew a 2½" x 10½" floral rectangle to the bottom of the unit. Then sew a 2½" x 12½" floral rectangle to the left side to complete the half block. Make a total of four of half block 2.

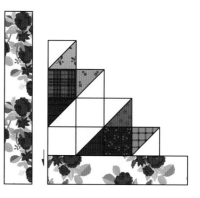

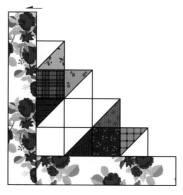

Half-block 2.
Make 4.

Corner Blocks

1. Sew light and dark squares together in pairs to make three half-square-triangle units. Press the seam allowances toward the dark triangles.

2. Lay out three half-square-triangle units, one dark square, and two light squares in two rows as shown. Sew the squares together in rows. Then sew the rows together. Make two and two reversed.

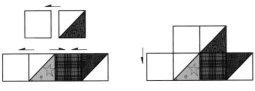

Make 2.

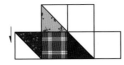

Make 2 reversed.

3. Fold a 2½" x 12½" floral rectangle in half and finger-press to mark the center. Matching the creased line and the center seam line in the unit, sew the rectangle to the bottom of the unit. Make two corner blocks and two reversed corner blocks.

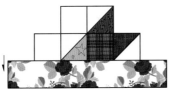

Make 2.

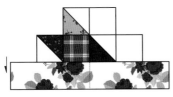

Make 2 reversed.

Assembling the Quilt Top

1. Lay out the blocks, half blocks, and corner blocks in diagonal rows as shown. Sew the blocks together in rows. Press the seam allowances in opposite directions from one row to the next. Then sew the rows together, matching the seam intersections. Press the seam allowances in one direction.

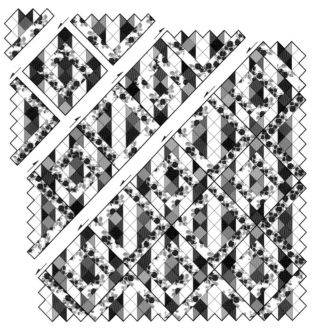

Quilt layout

2. With the *wrong side* of the quilt top facing up, trim the outer edges, leaving ¼" seam allowance beyond the crossed seams all the way around the quilt top.

Borders

For detailed instructions, refer to "Borders" on page 10.

1. For the inner border, sew the 2½"-wide dark strips end to end. Measure the width of your quilt. Cut two strips to this length and sew them to the top and bottom of the quilt top. Measure the length of your quilt top. Cut two strips to this length and sew them to the sides of the quilt top. Press the seam allowances toward the just-added borders.

2. In the same manner, measure, cut, sew, and press the 1½"-wide dark strips for the middle border. Then measure, cut, sew, and press the 4½"-wide floral strips for the outer border.

Finishing

For detailed instructions on finishing your quilt, refer to "Finishing Your Quilt" on page 10. Using the 2¼"-wide binding strips, make and attach binding.

10/18 ⑬ 1/17

Cheryl's personal philosophy about making quilts is simple—a quilt doesn't have to be perfect to be beautiful. She finds just as much joy in the creative process of quilting as in completing the project. Since starting her home-based business, "Country Quilts," in 2003, Cheryl has self-published over a hundred patterns and four books. She has exhibited her work at international quilt markets every year since then, and several of her designs have been published in national quilting magazines.

When she isn't designing and making quilts, Cheryl loves to create and seek out primitive treasures for her home. Traveling, antiquing, and spending time with family and friends are her other favorite pastimes. Cheryl and her husband, Ben, live in Abbotsford, British Columbia, Canada, in a house overflowing with quilts and crafts. Their two grown children, Charissa and Geoffrey, also live nearby. Cheryl is very thankful for her family and friends and that she is able to spend her days doing what she loves.

There's More Online!
See Cheryl's patterns, books, kits, and hand-dyed wool at www.countryquilts.ca.

Find more great books about quilting and more at www.martingale-pub.com.